JUGGLING
in high heels

Dear Sheryl,
enjoy!
love Lisa x

JUGGLING
in high heels

How to organise chaos

Lisa O'Neill

RANDOM HOUSE
NEW ZEALAND

CONTENTS

FOR MUM AND DAD

the best Big Elephants a
girl could ask for!

INTRODUCTION

The art of having it all

Oprah famously said 'You can have it all — just not all at once.'

I have always wanted it all. I guess that I am greedy by nature. For as long as I can remember I have wanted to be everything, have everything and do everything. I love the idea of being limitless. I love doing what I want, how I want, with whom I want. My nickname as a child was Princess Iwanta.

I was told by so many people that I couldn't do, have and be what I wanted. To that I say bollocks. I believe that it is our right as humans to be what we want. That we owe it to the universe to live the grandest, shiniest and most stunning life that we can muster — unless you don't want to be grand, shiny or stunning. You need to be what you want. Not what others want. Not what your teachers and parents wanted. What *you* want. You need to be yourself. All of yourself. Fully you.

Now, if you are anything like me, being fully yourself is a huge job. It is a 24/7 hanging-onto-the-rail-trying-to-keep-things-vertical kind of job. My life is big. It is tiring but it is amazing. But it is exactly how I want it: fabulous and full.

Now, you may not want a huge, full life. Maybe you want to go and lie under a rock and hide. Or maybe you do not know what you want — in which case I suggest you have a really big think about it.

In the busy-ness of life we often stop thinking. We stop wondering. We stop being curious about 'what if?' and 'maybe . . .'. We are so busy doing boring, everyday stuff that we have lost our ability to open our minds to huge and beautiful possibilities. 'Can't' becomes our default setting. I can't afford it. I can't find the time. I can't be bothered.

'What would you do if you knew you could not fail?' is one of my favourite questions. It is a great question, because it gets rid of all the crap. It takes away the thoughts like I don't have time, I am not good enough, it might not work, I'd probably fail, and I don't have the talent, and it lets us imagine. Imagine a limitless world. Just for a minute!

If you were guaranteed success, what would you choose to do? There is gold in your answer. There is something there worth looking into further.

I have a deep belief that I was born to succeed. I am pretty sure it came from my father. He has spent my whole life telling me that I can achieve anything. 'You can do anything you put your mind to' was his mantra, and one I will be forever grateful for. Both my brother and I look at things and think 'how can this work?' rather than 'will it work?'. It is a slightly different angle, but one that makes all the difference.

As a child I remember wanting to be a florist. Mostly I remember just wanting to do everything. I would see a woman with a large family and I would think 'I want to have lots of kids'. I would see a woman wearing a suit and carrying a briefcase and I would think 'I want to be a businesswoman'. I would watch the TV and I would think 'I want to be on TV'. I literally wanted it all. And I have it.

I have a huge, full and fun life. And I have this life because I made it happen. I didn't listen to the people who said I couldn't. I just thought about how I could do things. I believe that anything you have an urge to do, you can do. As Jesse Jackson famously said, 'If my mind can conceive it, and my heart can believe it, I know I can achieve it.'

I believe that if you have a desire to do something, then somewhere inside you is the ability to make that thing happen. It may not happen instantly, it mightn't happen tomorrow — but if you stick to it, it will bloom. The things we want to do hold clues for us. The answers are in the doing. Doing things that we want. That is what will lead you to your life's pot of gold.

Maybe you want to be a famous singer, but you can't sing. But the fact that you want to sing is gold. Go get some singing lessons. Join a choir. The point of the question 'What would you do if you knew you could not fail?' is not that you are going to be a famous singer. The point is that when you took away all the reasons why it wouldn't work you came up with the realisation that you wanted to sing.

This book is about doing what you want. It is about doing a lot.

Doing a lot takes a lot of work. Planning is the key. Working out your priorities is the way to start living your life on purpose.

This book is about living on purpose. It's about learning to juggle the things that are important and ditching the rest.

I hope this book helps you to do more. To be more. To have everything that you want. Maybe you don't want much — and that's OK. Maybe you are just overwhelmed by this large ocean of life. So let's start paddling.

Lisa x

CHAPTER ONE

What are you doing with your life?

DOING THE JUGGLE

My life is a juggle. And every day it's a different juggle. Most days, most of us find it hard to keep all our balls in the air. I see so many women who are exhausted, depleted, sleep-deprived, over-committed and unhappy. It is no wonder that divorce, depression and disconnection are a part of so many of our lives.

Many people feel that because they are doing so many things, they are not doing a great job at anything. They are under-parenting, not doing their best at work, feel like a bad friend, aren't looking after their health and have no money!

In my mentoring work, I always ask my clients at the very beginning to rate these things in their lives out of 10:

- mind
- body
- partner
- kids
- work
- friends
- money
- extended family.

Their responses tell me a lot. Try it for yourself. It is important that you write down the number that comes into your head first — not a number that you have created after thinking about it for 10 minutes!

Mind

- Is your head feeling scattered? Can you not think straight?
- Are you forgetful?
- Do you feel sad, anxious or worried?

Body

- Is your body sore and stiff?
- Are you physically exhausted?
- When was the last time you had an early night?

Partner

- Do you feel angry or guilty every time you think about your partner?
- Are they supportive?
- Do you give them enough time?

Kids

- Are your kids out of control?
- Are they in a difficult phase?
- Do they need more time? Do you need more rules?
- Do you need to give them some space?
- Are you making short-term decisions to keep everyone happy?

Work

- Are there never enough hours in the day?
- Do you feel valued?
- Are you bored?

Friends

- Do you wish you had more time to hang out with friends?
- Would you like to meet new people?
- Do you have friends who are weighing you down?

Money

- Are you worried about money?
- Do you need to be more organised with your money?
- Do you have large bills to pay and no idea where the money is going to come from?

Family

- Are you responsible for the care of your parents or other family members?
- Do you enjoy the company of your siblings and their families?
- Do you see too much/not enough of your extended family?

I answer these questions myself at least once a week. I like to jot down my responses on paper — seeing the numbers seems to make them more real. I then ask myself what I can do to improve the areas where I scored low.

There is a huge difference between what you *could* do and what you *can* do. Could do covers anything — can do is about what resources you have at your disposal. You *could* pay all your bills — if you had the money. Work on the *can*. What *can* I do about this? Right here, right now, with what I've got.

I have learnt to be gentle with myself with this process. It is not a beat-up session, where you tell yourself off for not being good enough. It is simply a check-in. Checking in with the different roles that you have and how they are going. Sometimes we can go weeks or years without giving certain areas of our lives conscious attention. Then a crisis hits and you realise there were things that you could have done to avoid it.

WHAT ARE YOUR ROLES?

We all do so much, care so much and love so much. When you make a list of all the roles that you have in life you will soon understand why your life feels so crazy! Here is an example of some roles you might have in different parts of your life:

Employee: You owe hours to someone in exchange for money.
Mother: You are responsible for the emotional and physical wellbeing of children.
Partner: You love and honour another person.
Friend: You are kind and thoughtful and fun.
Sister: You are best friend, confidante, supporter.
Daughter: You are kind and helpful and supportive.
Aunty/niece: You are kind and helpful and supportive.
Businesswoman: You are assertive, clever and responsible.
Colleague: You are supportive and helpful.
Volunteer: You are selfless and helpful.

Many of us have so many of these roles. I was at a workshop one day with a male friend, and we were discussing all the roles we had. My friend had no living parents, two sisters who lived miles away, no children and no partner.

When we compared our role lists he was blown away by how much I had on my plate! He then understood why I was not always available to attend shows and concerts and all the things that filled his life.

But this is not a competition! There are no prizes for having the most roles — trust me, I tried to win that medal and it never presented itself! There are so many women racing around, over-stuffing their diaries, desperately hoping that someone will notice and say 'Wow, aren't you amazing!'

We are all amazing. Doing more won't make you more amazing. Doing stuff you love will make you amazing. Amazingly happy, amazingly fun and just amazing to be around. Doing everything will turn you into a dramatic pain in the arse. Constantly complaining about all the shit that you have signed yourself up for is not to be admired!

I have always seen managing my roles as being like juggling balls. I currently have seven balls in the air. I'm a mother, sister, wife, friend, daughter, aunty/niece and businesswoman.

Juggling seven of anything is difficult. The secret is to only juggle what you need to on each given day. Put the other balls down. Most days I go to the highest bidder — the ball that bounces the highest usually gets the most attention!

Stephen Covey, in his book *The 7 Habits of Highly Effective People*, talks about the four types of tasks:

- Urgent and important — deadlines, meetings, crises.
- Important but not urgent — family, relationships, health.
- Urgent but not important — usually interruptions and dramas.
- Not important, not urgent — watching TV, social media, junk mail.

He suggests that we should always be focused on category two: the important but not urgent. Category four is where so many of us waste time. TV and social media can easily soak up three hours each day — that is 136 working days a year! Imagine what you could achieve if you stopped hanging out in category four!

Category three often occurs when we get caught in other people's drama, when other people's lack of planning becomes our problem. Try to avoid this category.

Unfortunately, category one cannot be avoided. Shit happens. We have all forgotten important dates, have had to stuff last-minute things into our lives or have had the rug pulled out from under us with accident or injury.

Category two is where we ideally want to live, working on the important stuff *proactively* — not urgently.

WHEN URGENT HAPPENS!

In 2009, I was in the middle of a large round of speaking events. I arrived home on a Friday night and noticed something wasn't right with my seven-year-old daughter, Tilly. She was very emotional, had lost quite a lot of weight and was constantly thirsty. On the Monday I was flying to Invercargill for another week of events. I decided to take her to the doctor before I left, just for some peace of mind.

My GP checked out Tilly and said she was probably just growing and not to be too concerned. I mentioned that I had read that the symptoms of Type 1 diabetes were weight loss, being thirsty and grumpy, etc. He said that she would be very sick if she had Type 1 diabetes, so he doubted it. But as we left the office we walked past a desk with a blood-sugar meter on it and he said 'We could do a quick blood-sugar reading if you are concerned?'

The reading was 28.6. The doctor went white and the nurse grabbed me and asked if I needed a hug. I had no idea what that meant — I asked if it was a good number. (I now know that normal blood sugars sit between 4 and 6!)

We were told we needed to get to hospital ASAP. They offered to call us an ambulance but I still didn't understand what a big deal this was about to be. We were met in the car park by a paediatric nurse and were rushed straight in. I realised then that Invercargill was not going to happen.

All my other balls were dropped. Tilly was now the only ball that I was holding tight in my hands. The other children's activities were put on hold, all other commitments were cancelled and we spent two weeks trying to learn how to keep our daughter alive.

The day we left the hospital, the doctor asked me how I felt about dealing with the daily performance of diabetes management. I told him that I was fine. I had felt quite comfortable about it all while I was holed up in this little room with one child, no work, no phone and nothing else to focus on. My challenge was going to be how I would be able to draw up an insulin needle while the phone was ringing, the cat was jumping on the bench and two of the other children were fighting! It took months to get the other balls back up in the air.

When urgent happens, it is incredible how kind and supportive people can be. But it shows us that even our best-laid plans sometimes don't come off. You cannot predict what curveball the world is going to throw at you. All we can do is plan for what we know we have to deal with.

So now that you know your roles, have a think about how much time each of them takes.

Most of us are awake for 112 hours each week. That is 16 hours each day — working on the theory that you have immaculate sleep habits and are in bed for 8 hours each night! For the sake of my very bad maths, let's round that down to 100.

If you work 40 hours a week, spend 7 hours travelling and around 20 hours each week eating, cooking and showering, that gives you 33 working hours left over each week. Nearly 5 hours a day. What are you doing with that time? Are you busy with a hobby? Playing sport? Watching TV? At children's activities? Helping an elderly relative? Shopping?

Working out where we spend our time is very useful. It will show you how full each of your roles is.

Write down your roles and keep a diary for a few weeks to see where you are spending your time.

CHAPTER TWO

Keeping your balls in the air

Think of each of the roles in your life as a ball. Some are heavy, some are bouncy, some are soft. Some are more important than others. Some are precious. Some balls are crystal — like the teenage daughter ball. Drop *that* one and there will be a mess! Tears, drama, chaos and likely a nasty memory that will be thrown in your face when she is 30.

Some balls are bouncy and healthy, and if you leave them unattended for a moment nothing too dramatic will take place. Others you need to keep your eye on at all times.

Each kid, each project, each relationship is a ball. The key is awareness and selection — awareness of the current state and needs of each ball, and selection of which balls you are going to have up in the air at any one time.

Awareness: in order to be helpful, supportive and loving to the people that we care about in our lives, we need to have some awareness around them.

Selection: this can be tough. You need to decide which balls need the most attention and which ones you are going to place back in your juggler's box for a bit.

So, let's look at your balls . . . !

BALL ONE: ME! ME! ME! IT'S ALL ABOUT ME!

You are important. Having a 'me' ball will stop you from becoming bitter and depleted. The 'me' ball is all about the things that make you happy, all the things that help you to feel great, to be the best version of you.

Being tired, grumpy and unhappy will not give you a great life. You will, quite honestly, just be a pain in the arse. You children will not want to hang out with you, your partner will not want to come home and your friends will be in the past tense.

If you read nothing else in this book, please read this!

You are responsible for the quality of your life. You. No one else. Yes, you might have had bad experiences, you might have had bad luck, but you are the only person who has any hope of getting it sorted.

You are responsible for the quality of your life.

BEING SELFISH?

When I discuss self-care with women, their first comment is often that they would feel 'selfish' taking an hour out to have a massage or to do something for themselves. They have been brainwashed that spending time on themselves must take away from what they can do for others.

In fact, the opposite is true. When we spend time on ourselves we become better, we become more. We have more energy, love and enthusiasm to give others.

I think the word selfish is often used incorrectly. The dictionary states that it means 'lacking consideration for others'. I completely disagree. If something is described as 'yellowish', it means that it is somewhat yellow. If something is 'childish', it means that it is like or appropriate for a child. If someone is described as 'boyish', then they look or act like a young man. So to me, this means that to be 'selfish' is to be like or appropriate to yourself. Being selfish is to be more like yourself.

So what can you do to be more like yourself? When I sleep well or have a holiday I often feel more like myself. When I run myself ragged and hear myself yelling at everyone around me, being short-tempered and angry, I am nothing like my 'self' that I know I can be.

So let's get a selfish list going — a list of things that will make you feel more like yourself.

- When do you feel amazing? Is it early in the morning? Late at night? After exercise?
- Where do you feel amazing? Is it lying in the sun? Is it at the beach? Is it in the bath?
- What makes you feel amazing? Is it when you are dressed up? When you have eaten a healthy meal? When you have lots of time?

Make your life selfish — arrange everything for your own advantage and pleasure. You job is to be more of yourself — not to eat burnt chops . . .

We need to learn to put ourselves first if we are going to end up anywhere but last.

BURNT CHOP SYNDROME

Dinner is not an easy thing to pull off. And every time you get it over with, there is another opportunity coming to feed everyone again!

Deciding what to cook can be paralysing for many women. Let's face it — presenting the family with the evening meal is rarely met with a universally positive response. In our house there seems to be a constant flow of complaints, 'ew yuck' and 'I don't like . . .'. It seems impossible to put a meal in front of six people aged 4 to 46 and get an overwhelming sense of gratitude — except for when I serve the good old roast (gets them every time!).

The parent who produces the meal — first deciding what to cook, then dealing with the supermarket, then the preparing and planning, then the actual slaving over the stove — often suffers from something I call Burnt Chop Syndrome.

I watched my mother as I was growing up. After several hours of effort she would serve herself the worst piece, the smallest portion or the bit that she was not happy to give anyone else. She'd say, 'Put it on my plate.'

This putting-ourselves-last behaviour needs to stop.

I have always come at dinner from a different angle. If I am the person who is selecting, buying, preparing and cooking the meal, I will give myself the bits that I want — the crispiest piece of chicken, the plumpest chop. Why wouldn't you?

You wouldn't, because you see this act of service as loving. And it is — but not to you.

No one else is going to look after you. No one else is going to offer you the best cut of meat.

BALL TWO: YOUR HEALTH IS YOUR WEALTH

This is another ball we often forget about, but it is a crucial one to not drop. At some stage we have all dropped our health ball, ignored something, got sick. It's not fun. A bit of effort now can save you a lot of time and energy later.

ASK YOURSELF:

- How is my health in general?
- Do I get enough sleep?
- What do I eat in large quantities? (Our bodies often crave what they shouldn't have. I was once told by a very wise naturopath that the food group you crave the most is the thing you shouldn't have. What could you not live without? Ice cream? Coffee? Bread? Alcohol?)
- What could I do to improve my health?
- What do I need to attend to — check-ups and health appointments?
- Who is in my health team? Massage therapist/osteopath/nutritionist/personal trainer/healer?

I am a huge believer in the benefits of massage and reiki. Putting some loving kindness back into my busy, tired body is just what it needs after it has been stuffed into planes, trains and automobiles most weeks. Massage is good for your stress levels, your muscles, your skin and your mind. There really is nothing nicer than being rubbed by someone who doesn't want anything in return! Some people are very strange about being touched — but being touched will help you get in touch with your body. Don't worry about being too fat, too hairy or too whatever else you have decided . . . massage therapists see bodies all day, every day and can help you to get in touch with yours.

EXERCISE, ANYONE?

What type of exercise does your body enjoy? I hate cardio exercise — I get red hot and it hurts! People talk to me about endorphins and the 'buzz' they get from going on a run or a two-hour bike ride. No, thank you! A stretch at yoga, some dancing, a gentle swim or a walk through some trees does it for me. Small bike seats and running when no one is chasing me seems like a waste of my life!

We all know what we 'should' be doing for the good of our health, and yet so few people do what they 'should'. I think the secret is to take what we 'should' be doing and turn it into a 'want'.

Instead of feeling like you 'should' exercise, imagine the difference if you 'wanted' to exercise.

'Should' is such an awful word — I like 'want' way more!

Humans seem to have a huge ability to self-sabotage. Imagine how great our lives would be if we did everything that we know we 'should' do for the greater good of our bodies.

Our bodies have simple needs. They need fuel, rest, movement and hydration. Why is it so hard to give them these things? Why do we fill our bodies with crap food, not drink enough water and stay up half the night?

Warning — I am going to get deep here. My theory on this is that we lack self-love. If we truly loved and respected ourselves, we wouldn't sabotage our precious bodies. It's like we sabotage our bodies in an effort to reduce our chance of having an incredible life. Because we don't actually believe that we deserve to have everything we want.

Learning to understand and respect our bodies needs to be taught in schools. Our bodies are incredible. They are magnificent, self-healing devices that offer us so much, and how do we repay them? By forcing bad food, bad habits and bad lifestyles on them.

ASK YOURSELF:

- If I truly loved myself, how would I treat my body?
- What would my week include if I was doing everything I could out of self-love for my body?
- What would I eat?
- How would I move?
- How much would I sleep?

Learning to love and care for your body is a lot of work. If you need help, there is plenty around. There are so many wonderful body-care experts in the world. I am not talking about doctors and specialists and people who fix medical problems. I am talking about proactive wellness.

Naturopaths, iridologists, osteopaths, nutritionists and chiropractors are all great people to start with. They are trained to read your body and can offer advice on how to get the best out of it.

When we do things proactively for our bodies, it is like active health insurance. It's a way better approach than waiting until something goes wrong before we take some action.

It is very easy to find ourselves depleted by our busy lives. Many of the women I meet at my events are totally depleted. You can see it in their eyes.

They are five minutes away from bursting into tears. They are mentally, emotionally or nutritionally depleted. Mentally they are tired from being responsible for so much, emotionally they are depleted from not feeling adequately supported, nutritionally they are depleted from not stocking their bodies with the goodness that they need.

Their lives are so busy, they are constantly overwhelmed and they 'don't have time' to address their issues. They spend years being everything to everyone and nothing to themselves. Then they wonder why they feel like shit!

So many women in this shut-down state get diagnosed with depression. I hear stories of women feeling overwhelmed or unhappy who turn up at their GP and get offered a quick fix in the form of a pill. Now, I fully understand that medication can be a huge help for some people, and that mental illness is not something that should be taken lightly, but so many women end up in a medical cycle because they are offered an instant cure rather than looking at the areas of their lives where they need support. I am not suggesting that people with mental-health diagnoses can be cured with a multi-vitamin and an early night, but so many women who turn up at the doctor's office in this state are 'depleted', not depressed.

If they were mentally stimulated by something they were passionate about, emotionally nurtured by someone who cared, and getting the daily recommended doses of sleep, vitamins and minerals, they would not need these quick fixes. I think that it pays to check these three areas before heading down the medical intervention route.

Have a blood test to check your hormones, vitamin B and iron levels. Get your thyroid checked. Take a few days off. Give yourself the benefit of four early nights in a row. Drop everything and do something that makes your heart sing. Give yourself a break — step out of your daily life and visit a friend. Just two days away can refresh and renew your perspective.

A quick trip to the doctor might seem like an easy fix, but it can end in a lifetime of medical dependency. I love the level of awareness now around mental health, and the brave people who speak openly about the difficulties that they live with. The downside is that the minute you tell someone that you aren't coping or are feeling overwhelmed, these days they want to label you as depressed.

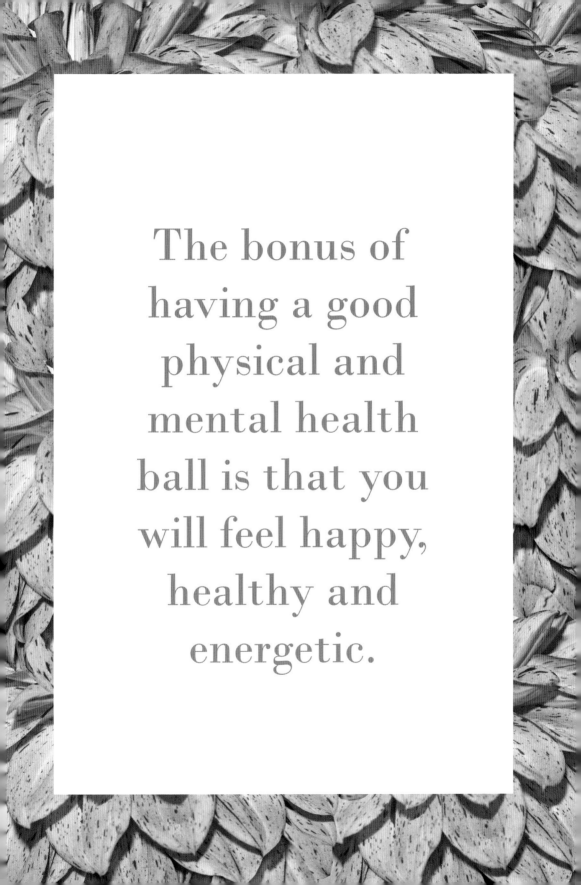

The bonus of having a good physical and mental health ball is that you will feel happy, healthy and energetic.

BALL THREE: THE LOVE OF YOUR LIFE

ASK YOURSELF:

- How much time do I spend with my partner?
- What does my partner need from me?

It is likely that, over time, this person has gone from being the number one thing in your life to being about number five down the list! But no matter how many other things you are juggling, you need to honour your relationship. Make time. Make sure that your diary and your life reflect how important your partner is to you. Honour them and insist that they honour you in turn.

It is really easy to neglect your partner. But you don't want to wake up one day and find that they have left and you didn't even notice! Do something nice each day for them, say something nice to them, go out of your way to do thoughtful things for them.

But make sure these are things that make *them* happy . . . and don't waste your time doing things that they do not care about. For years I bought my husband presents. I like presents and so I assumed everyone did. I would give him a gift and it would sit unopened! I couldn't understand it until I read *The Five Love Languages* by Gary D Chapman. It changed my life.

In the book, Gary talks about five different ways to express your love for someone. Each person has a primary love language — gifts, quality time, acts of service, physical touch and words of affirmation. As a 'gifter', it seemed right to me that others would like gifts — wrong!

Think about what makes your partner happy. Is it a gift? Is it some one-on-one time? Is it someone putting out the rubbish or making them a coffee? Is it a back rub or cuddle? Or is it a note, or you telling them how much you appreciate them? Working out other people's love languages can improve all your relationships and save you lots of time and effort. There is no point going shopping for an expensive gift if they are happy with the rubbish being put out! (For more on this, see page 39.)

Maybe you don't have a significant other. In that case, this ball can be about spending some time searching for someone new. If you are a woman who teaches six-year-olds all day and who spends every living minute at work, then chances are the only person you are going to find to date is a six-year-old!

Life is not a movie. Partners do not drop out of the sky. If you want milk, you have to go to the dairy. Think about what you want in a partner and go to where those people are. Do you want a sporty guy? Head to a sports match. Do you want an intellectual? Go to the library. You can't catch a fish without a line . . . If having a partner is important to you, then make it happen. Get moving.

The first time I saw my husband, Mark, I was 14 years old. I was walking past the tennis courts with my friend Tracey and I turned to her and said 'I'm going to marry him.' She laughed at me and said 'He'll never talk to you.' She was right! He doesn't talk — but I don't need him to talk. I have plenty of people to talk to! But I did marry him. I effectively followed him around for four years trying to get him to notice me. My persistence paid off!

Mark and I don't actually have a lot in common. He is quiet, I am noisy. He loves sport, I hate it. He is dark, I am blonde. He is a thinker, I am a doer. He is the introvert, I am the extrovert.

The secret of our relationship has actually been our differences. Because we have never had anything in common, we have never tried to force each other to be what we are not.

I absolutely believe that separateness can create closeness. Sometimes being apart is the answer to feeling more together. When you are both busy and fulfilled, you will meet up in a happy place. If one of you is needy and dependent, it will push the other away. Always be responsible for your 50 per cent or the relationship.

Mark and I balance each other out. He is brilliant at all the stuff I am bad at, and I am great at all the stuff he hates. Perfect! Together we are the complete package.

I think that the purpose of any relationship is to enhance and grow each other. And you need to love one another unconditionally. True love has no interest in control. True love wants to see the other flourish and be happy. People in relationships who want to 'fix' each other will get very little benefit.

Picking the right person is vital. In fact, picking the right partner is one of the biggest choices you will ever make. If you choose badly you can open up your life to a lot of misery. Financial stress and emotional dysfunction are not things that you want to sign yourself up for.

Although Mark and I apparently had nothing in common, our families were quite similar. Both of us grew up in families where the mother was the primary caregiver and both our fathers were self-employed businessmen. So without realising it we both had similar ways of thinking and theories about families and raising children.

I remember when all our friends were getting married, one couple had to go to 'marriage lessons' with their priest. I mocked them, laughing at how I couldn't believe that they were going to get lessons on how to be married from someone who wasn't allowed to marry themselves!

But the lessons were hugely valuable. The priest asked them about their own families and childhoods. One of them had a working mother who was also an artist and led a very busy social life, while the other had a stay-at-home mum who had sacrificed her whole life to 'be there for her children'. When they were asked how they each saw their roles as future parents they realised that they had some big issues to discuss.

The funny things about humans is that we all think that whatever we do is normal. So if your mum worked full-time then that is normal to you. If your husband's mother was a stay-at-home mum then he will consider that normal. It doesn't matter if you have had different experiences, but I think talking about these things is vital.

Do you want to have children? How many? Do you want to take time out of your career to be at home?

———

After children, money and sex are the two other big issues that most couples have to face.

When I met Mark, all either of us owned were bikes and a school uniform. There was no need for a pre-nup! We had nothing and, like many young couples, everything we created we created together.

Money can be a big issue if your money values are not the same. If one person loves to save money and values their security, then being with someone who shops constantly and has lots of debt will throw the relationship into a spin. In modern times, many couples run their finances completely

independently, with both contributing to household costs. I know one couple where the husband pays his wife $55,000 per year to be at home looking after their children! He told me that his life was easier when the kids' needs were met, and so that his wife felt valued he thought she should have an income that reflected her role. She then also had her own income and did not have to feel that awful feeling of having no money of 'her own'.

Having clear and honest discussions about money will always help a relationship. Secrets never work.

Make a plan. Have financial focus. Sometimes the focus is just to pay the bills. If you have surplus cash, decide what to do with it. Family holiday? Reducing debt?

Think of yourselves as two board directors — each with equal power. What is in the best interests of your company (the family)? What will benefit the customers (your children)?

Money focuses change depending on where you are at in your life. If one parent is at home while the children are young, then there may not be the money for extras. Remember, it's not forever. Just keep talking.

And the old saying that men need sex to feel loved and women need love to feel like sex is so true! Men love friction. Women love romance. We are wired so very differently.

Remember the early days when you couldn't get enough of each other? Like all other aspects of your relationship, having a good sex life also takes effort. Making an effort to make time for your partner, to look good for your partner and to please your partner is very worthwhile.

I know making this kind of effort is not easy when you have a young family. After the rollercoaster of pregnancy and birth, many women struggle with bringing back their sexy selves. It becomes just another job to do! Being constantly tired and having children hanging off your body does not do much to help you feel sexy.

In turn, men feel ripped off. They can get resentful and feel locked out. Their beautiful wife has a new love and suddenly has no time for them.

It's hard to feel sexy when you hate your body — no, it probably doesn't look like it did before you had a tenant move into your building and mess the place up! But *trust* your body.

When you are feeling fat and exhausted and 'sexless', you might feel like the only person that this has ever happened to. You are not! Talk to your

friends. Other women will get it. I have a funny friend who always wants to discuss money and sex — she is amazed at how both things play such a big part in our lives and yet very few people discuss them.

Feeling relaxed will make you feel way more sexy than being an uptight robot! Non-sexual touch is vital during these times. Many women are scared to reach out to their husband 'in case he wants more', and men can give up after being shut down at each approach.

I believe that we are all sexual beings and that our sexual self is too important to ignore. There will be times when you would just prefer a cup of tea and a good book . . . but make an effort. People who have regular sex are happier and healthier than those who don't.

Mark and I have now been together for nearly 30 years but when he walks into a room I still think 'I'd do him', which is a great way to look at your partner. In order to play the long game I think you need some strategies to keep your relationship alive.

Focus on what you love

Constantly bringing your attention to the things that you love about your partner is a much better strategy than bitching about all the things that drive you nuts. We all have annoying habits and personality traits. If you focus on your partner's shortcomings, you will drive yourself out of the relationship real fast!

Magnifying their good bits is the way to go. Turn a blind eye to the annoying things and magnify the hell out of the stuff you like.

What attracted you to your partner when you first met? What is your favourite thing that they do? What do you love about them?

Stop focusing on the shoes he leaves in the hallway and the dishes he puts in the sink instead of the dishwasher. Start looking for the things he is good at, the things that he does well.

Long-term love is not easy. You have to stay engaged. You need to stay interested. You will get bored. You will get frustrated. I cannot believe people who actually assume that merging your life with another human until one of you dies is ever going to be easy!

Do nice things

When was the last time you did something thoughtful for your partner? When was the last time they did something thoughtful for you?

Many men have no idea what women want, and yet we expect them to magically know. If you want your partner to buy you flowers or to take you out on a date, then tell them. Do not default to being the bitching victim. People are not mind-readers and you will be bitterly disappointed if you expect all your needs to be met without expressing them first. Stomping around in a bad mood is no way to behave if you are in an adult relationship.

Ask your partner what you can do for them to make their day or week better. Then tell them what you need from them.

In my experience, men are delighted when we tell them what we want. We confuse the hell out of them, and many are left with the feeling that nothing that they do is ever going to be right.

Being in service to the happiness of your partner is a brilliant way to treat your relationship. But it only really works if your partner is also in service to *your* happiness!

If your partner has no investment in your life, then you really have to ask yourself what you are getting out of the relationship. They might say that they love you but actions speak louder than words. What do their actions say?

Speak nicely to each other

It shocks me how some couples speak to each other, especially older couples. Being together for 40 years does not give you licence to speak to the other like they are a factory second. Negative remarks, constantly correcting the things they are doing wrong and trying to look good at the expense of your partner is not cool.

How you speak *about* your partner is as important as how you speak *to* them. Constantly putting them down and broadcasting their faults is not going to make either of you feel very fabulous.

Where attention goes, energy flows. Put your energy into what you love about them and tell everyone. Tell people what a fantastic father he is. Tell your mother what a great cook he is. I know women who think that it's cool to bitch about their man — they think it makes them look better.

If you don't like him, then leave, but do not ruin someone's life while you live with them. If you are in, then be all in. Speak nice, do nice, play nice.

This goes the other way as well. Do not put up with people who speak badly to you or put you down — you deserve better.

Keep your eye on the prize

What is the point of your relationship? Some people want to entwine their lives together because they cannot live apart. Some people want to raise a family. Some just want someone to pay half of the mortgage!

There are many reasons people get together and stay together. Financial reasons, family reasons and some just because they are madly in love. I want to be an old grey-haired lady who travels and laughs and enjoys her husband's company. What's your end goal?

Raising a family is a big job. It takes stamina and strength and a commitment of support. Keeping a focus on you as a couple will help get you out the other end. Parenting is not forever (though it can feel like it sometimes!).

Someone once told me that the greatest gift I could give my children was to love their father. Sometimes it takes work to love the person who is under your feet all the time; sometimes it takes effort that you simply do not have.

If you are looking for someone to start a family with, look very hard. The person you choose will have a huge impact on how successful your family unit will be.

Love is a verb

A verb is a doing word. To get the most out of love you have to 'do' love, to actually *feel* deep affection for someone.

You have to actually practise this. You cannot just walk past each other and expect an overwhelming gush of love. Once again, life is not a movie!

Ask yourself what you can do that is an act of love for your partner. Verbalise what they can 'do' for you. Consciously 'doing love' will hugely benefit your relationship.

The bonus of
having a good
partner ball is
that you will feel
loved, supported
and honoured
and respected
in return.

MARRIAGE ADVICE FROM 1886

Let your love be stronger
than your hate or anger.

Learn the wisdom of compromise, for it
is better to bend a little than to break.

Believe the best rather than the worst.

Remember, people have a way of living
up or down to your opinions of them.

Remember also that true friendship is
the basis for any lasting relationship.

The person you choose to marry
is deserving of the courtesies and
kindnesses you bestow on your friends.

Please hand this down to your children
and your children's children,
for the more things change
the more they remain the same.

— Jane Wells

LOVE LANGUAGES

The idea of love languages was created by Gary Chapman, in his book *The Five Love Languages*. Getting your head around these five languages is a great way to save time, by doing things that actually mean something for other people rather than what you assume would make them happy.

Most of us are a combination of the five languages — obviously we all would like people to make time for us, to say lovely things to us, to buy us gifts, to do kind things and give us loving hugs, but two of the five will be more important to you than the other three.

There are five people in my home that I want to keep happy, and learning about the five love languages has helped me to do just that.

The five types are:

Gift giving: Some people love to give and be given gifts — but it is more about the thought behind the gift than the value. This language can be mistaken for materialism, but it is really the effort and the thought going into the giving that is the exciting bit. Finding the perfect gift for someone makes my heart explode with joy.

Acts of service: My husband Mark's language is acts of service. Nothing makes him happier than doing things for others and other people doing things for him. Making him a coffee, filling the car with gas, picking up something from town — these little acts of service mean so much to him.

Physical touch: One of my sons has always been very big on physical touch and affection. People whose love language is physical touch are usually very tuned-in to body language and they energise themselves by drawing on the physical energy of others.

Words of affirmation: My daughter is big on words. She will often write me notes, and sends text messages for no other reason than to say hi. Not very good with criticism, these people like to be listened to, and they love compliments!

Quality time: These people crave uninterrupted conversations and time set aside exclusively for them. Having four children to juggle, this one is a biggie for me. I try to take them individually to places just so we can get that time without another one butting in or competing for some attention. Planning outings especially for them is the greatest way to fill up their tanks.

People usually do for others what they want others to do for them. This is a helpful clue in working out what their love language is.

BALL FOUR: STAYING MUM

The number of children you have will define how many balls you have in this category. When children are little, you can pop them all in one ball: 'The Kids'. As they grow, they will each require their very own ball — a space for all their quirks and weirdness and different activities!

The child ball can become very fragile at different times. In my experience they are:

1. During life-changing events — birth/death/marriage/divorce.

2. Starting school or changing school.

3. During illness or medical issues.

4. Boys aged 14–16.

5. Girls aged 11–16.

6. Leaving school.

7. Relationship break-ups.

Children are constantly changing and have different needs every day. Because I am away from home a lot, it is vital to me that I know where each of my kids is at.

ASK YOURSELF:

- How is Child X?
- What is going on for them at the moment?
- What is coming up for them at the moment?
- What would they say is their biggest issue right now? (And this may be different to what *you* think is their biggest issue!)
- What is one important thing that I can do for them?

Children need two types of care:

1.   Physical care: food/bath/transport/toenails . . .

2.   Emotional care: mind/self-worth/heart-space.

The physical care aspect gets easier as children get older. In the beginning there are high chairs and car seats, shoelaces to tie and swimming lessons to attend. Later it seems to be just a sandwich and a car ride and some cash. Physical care is busy, but this can be outsourced. Daycare, nanny, grandparents and friends are all great helpers here.

Emotional care is the ball that many parents drop — or they are simply unaware of it until it is sitting in their lap, sobbing. Then they become drastically aware of it!

Children need time; time to talk, to decompress, to try to understand people's behaviour, their feelings and where they fit into the world. For me this is the important bit. Many parents spend loads of time on the food and the bath and not so much on the self-belief and emotional support.

Children are like plants. They need good nutrients, a healthy environment and sunshine.

I have now been a mother for 17 years. What a ride! Parenting has to be one of the hardest things that we ever do. Being a mother has so far been the most gorgeous, rewarding, frustrating and totally exhausting thing that I have ever done.

I have learnt that everything is a phase, that nothing lasts forever. I have learnt that we are guiding lights for these little people and can only do the best that we can at any time. I know what it feels like to totally sacrifice myself for others, and what it feels like when you have joy and pride oozing out your pores. Parenting is like surfing — sometimes it's calm, sometimes it's turbulent!

I think the job of parents is to create fully grown, independent, loved little humans who will contribute to society — not to breed useless, entitled little brats. It is very easy to do everything for them, to give them everything. Saying no is hard — I think it always has been, but there is just so much more to say no to these days.

Parenting in this day and age is busy. There is more to do than just feed and clothe them. Managing social-media accounts and cyber-safety are all additional responsibilities of the modern parent. The pressure of technology and the cost of international school trips puts so much pressure on families. 'In my day' we were happy if we went to Wellington on a bus — now schools send intermediate-aged children to Japan!

———————

When I first became a parent I felt like I had been given a beautiful mound of perfect playdough. I was going to sculpt this little life into everything I had dreamed of. I had dreams and plans and ideas for my little person. They were going to be perfect. And then they weren't. Then they decided they didn't want to do what I had planned. They had their own ideas!

I now have four humans that I am responsible for, each with their own set of ideas. Four completely different personalities who all have the same parents, the same address and have been raised the same way.

As Kahlil Gibran wrote in *The Prophet*:

Your children are not your children.
They are the sons and daughters of Life's longing for itself.
They come through you but not from you,
And though they are with you yet they belong not to you.
You may give them your love but not your thoughts,
For they have their own thoughts.
You may house their bodies but not their souls,
For their souls dwell in the house of tomorrow, which you cannot visit,
not even in your dreams.
You may strive to be like them, but seek not to make them like you.
For life goes not backward nor tarries with yesterday.
You are the bows from which your children as living arrows are sent forth.

This sums up my attitude to parenting. I believe that we are caretakers of our little people. They have their own thoughts — they do not belong to you — but still we must pay and provide.

I remember when I had my first baby I thought everything was so hard. People told me it would get worse, and I never believed them!

It does get worse. But it also gets better. There just seems to be a never-ending range of phases to juggle. Whether you are toilet-training or teaching them to drive or buying them condoms or teaching them to use a spoon — there is a never-ending list of things to do. There are problems to solve, stories to listen to and money to dish out. The hardest thing I find is knowing when to push and when to hold back.

It's a bit like that song 'The Gambler'. Something comes up and I think, should I give them a shove or a hug? Shall I make them go and sort that mess out for themselves or shall I be their soft place to land?

Often we get it wrong — afterwards you think 'I should never have agreed to this' or 'I should have gone easier' — but it's done. And all of us are just doing the best we can with what we have got.

Sometimes it is not much. Sometimes you feel so depleted that you actually have nothing to give — nothing to offer. Other times you blow it by over-servicing the problem.

The other huge problem with parenting is there are so many nosy, judgemental 'experts' who seem to be hovering around just waiting for you to screw something up so they can say they knew that was going to happen! The 'parenting police' are a tough crowd — sitting judging your kid while theirs is doing the exact same things but they are too blind or blinkered to see it.

Let them go. Make them a little paper boat and let the bastards float away! Revenge is a dish best served cold. Let the judgers judge. Haters gonna hate. Perfect parents and perfect children can go and live on their own island for all I care!

People who judge you constantly are also generally very hard on themselves. They are under the 'what will people think' spell. They are so worried about what other people think that they are extra-hard on both you and themselves. They will judge you at every turn.

If you're a mother, you're dammed if you do, dammed if you don't.

If you're a working mother you will be judged: the morning-tea makers will line up at the gate.

If you are a stay-at-home mother, the working mothers will dash past you in their heels, making you feel like crap.

I have been the stay-at-home mum and I have been the working mum — and both have their ups and downs. As the working mum you need a huge guilt shield — you need to deflect and protect yourself from all the guilt that you will feel as you are sprayed with judgement from other parents and school staff.

I had one mother tell me that she had always worked but she and her husband had decided that they wanted the best for their children, so they had decided she would stay home until they finished school. I wanted to say 'Yeah, Mark and I had a chat and have decided that we don't want the best for any of ours, so I went to work!' What a ridiculous comment! I know that she was merely justifying her at-home existence with her stupid ramble, but I really wish they would put signs up at school to stop the 'mother judges'!

Sometimes I really want to move to a planet where everyone just does their thing and no one gets in the way, looking down their tut-tut noses. The truth is that some mothers work, some mothers do not.

Some mothers who work do not want to work but they have to, to bring home some bacon.

Some mothers are at home, pretending to be homemaker of the year, when all they really want is a quiet office and a company credit card.

Some mothers are in love with homemaking. They cook, sew, bake and plait their children's hair. Good for them.

Do what makes you happy and your kids will get it. No child needs to be raised by an unhappy mother. A resentful mother who doesn't get to do anything for herself is no fun. Happy parents have happy kids. And you are the only person who can give your children a happy mother.

Boys and girls

I am the proud owner of two boys and two girls. I find the difference in parenting them is huge!

BOYS

When I had my eldest son, my best friend had a daughter of the same age. We were both first-time mothers and would spend hours comparing notes and milestones. Her daughter would sit still and play, and babbled out lots of words, while my son was always on the move and seemed to make only truck noises! He loved to jump on things and smash things up.

Now I know that this was as much his personality as his boyness. But I do think that mothers need to appreciate the difference between raising boys and raising girls.

I spent four years trying to make Oscar behave like a girl. Then I met a mother of four boys. Oscar went to play at their house and ended up jumping out of trees and covering himself in mud. When I picked him up he had had the time of his life. I realised that this was what he needed.

At five years old, Oscar started learning taekwondo. I firmly believe that all boys should practise a martial art. They get to play out all their fantasies of kicking and punching and jumping and being ninjas, in a safe and respectful environment.

Little girls get to role-play their fantasy worlds with dolls and dresses and yet we try to stop boys from exploring their fantasy worlds.

For example, I decided when Oscar was little that I was not going to allow him to have toy guns. I did not think that allowing him to practise killing people was a good idea. It was quite a fight. In the end Oscar made a gun one morning from his piece of toast and I let my silly rule go. Giving a four-year-old a toy gun will not turn him into a terrorist — having a mental mother might!

Teaching your boys to respect you and treat you well will go a long way towards them having a positive attitude to women when they grow up. Mothers who let their sons speak badly to them, hit them and treat them with no respect are doing their boys a huge disservice. You are teaching them to disrespect all women!

Eleven to fourteen years is a key time to keep boys happy, healthy and engaged. If they hit puberty with a strong sense of self and with some good role models, they will be OK. The late Celia Lashlie, boy expert extraordinaire, whom I had the pleasure of working with several times, wrote in her book *He'll Be OK*: 'Mothers need to stop expending energy in trying to make their sons into something that they are not. Women need to accept the reality of men rather than forever wanting to change it and them'.

After reading *He'll Be OK* and hearing Celia speak several times, I became convinced that my job as a mother of a son was primarily from birth to the age of 14. After that he needs males to take him over 'the bridge of adolescence'. Her book should be compulsory reading for any mothers raising boys.

GIRLS

Girls have a much more independent, 'I'll do it myself' kind of energy from boys. As women raising little women, I think we owe it to our daughters to be good role models. Show them how to be fulfilled and happy by being these things yourself.

If you are not very 'girly' and struggle with things like shopping and makeup, try learning with them. Get your eyebrows done together. Try to bond over what they are interested in. If you show no interest in what they are into they will take it that you are not interested in *them*.

I remember how hard it was to be a teenage girl: how raw the emotions were, how huge all my feelings seemed. On top of that you have body stuff, boy stuff, nasty-girl stuff — so much stuff.

So be gentle with your own girls. Explain to them that it's OK to feel awful — as hormonal creatures they will often have days where they want to kill people! They also need to know that if they can't manage their moods it is not OK to take it out on others. Suggest that they might be better off having some time alone rather than ruining the mood of the entire family!

The teenage years are a rocky road. Keep them close, know who they are, what they are doing and who their friends are. It's important that they know that you understand them. That you will fight for them. That you are on their team — not on the opposite side.

Working out who you are as a woman often involves some kind of pushing-off from your own mother. If you have a strong daughter, expect her to push off and rebel against who you are and what you stand for. It is a good sign that she has strength and character (even though it won't feel good at the time!). While they are trying to work out who they are and want to be, they may decide that they hate who *you* are . . . it's not personal. Pretend insults don't bother you and laugh them off. It will be way more powerful than fighting back.

Ten tips for parents

Do what's right, not what's easy. It's very tempting to give in and go with the easier option. Long-term this is not a good plan! But give yourself three 'get out of jail' cards each month that you can use to override the rules.

Move on. Deal with stuff that happens and then start the next day anew. Kids

do dumb things, so do adults. Don't hold grudges. Deal with stuff and start each day fresh.

Have a weekly plan on the fridge so everyone knows where everyone is. Each Sunday I write up the plan for the following week: who's going where, who is taking them, what is needed. Get all the information out of your head and onto a piece of paper and display it where everyone can take responsibility for it. Or you could have a weekly meeting to let everyone know what is going on and when. Start young and get children used to being briefed about the week's events. Tell them in advance if you have a huge week at work or if you are going to be away. Kids cope best when they are fully informed. Parents who lie and sneak out will lose their children's trust.

Plan meals the day before, and always have something cooked and ready go in the freezer. Getting home at 6 p.m. with no dinner plans is not ideal. When my children were little, whatever we ate, they ate it the next night. I would cook dinner and plate up little servings for the following night. That way the kids' dinner was only ever five minutes away.

Make an effort to greet your children every morning and when you get home at the end of the day. Mornings and evenings are great times to check in and reconnect. Taking time to snuggle in the mornings and evenings is vital, too. Record youself reading their favourite books on an iPad so they can have 'mummy time' if you are working late or away.

Teach them to be interested in other people. Children are very self-absorbed, and need to be taught to show an interest in other people's days and interests. I love hearing my kids asking each other about their days!

Give them some insight. Parents who let their children behave like idiots do them no favours. I bought my son a poster for his room that says 'Don't Be A Dick'. Just a friendly reminder! When your kid is being a dick, tell them. Otherwise they will end up with no sense of social reality. Learning to handle themselves is part of growing up, and teaching them how to handle situations is part of your parenting job. I see children who cannot handle losing a game or who are constantly jealous of others — they need to get over it. Someone

will always be better than you and have something that you think you want. As a parent, if you don't use these 'teachable' moments to help your child grow then you are doing them a disservice.

Educate them about food. In order to grow up as healthy humans, they need to understand good nutrition. Explain what nutrients do for your body and what foods have which nutrients. We used to play a game of 'How many colours did you eat?' at dinner. We each had to list all the different-coloured foods we had eaten during the day — it opened up a lot of discussion about the benefits of different foods. Make sure that your kids can cook. High-protein snacks like scrambled eggs are a far better option than large bags of chippies after school.

Tell them what you love about your job. Don't whinge to them about your life. Kids don't need lectures about how hard 'adulting' is. By living a happy, fulfilled life you will inspire them to do the same.

Find a good, non-judgemental friend who you can unload on and share your triumphs and disasters with. Parenting is tough and you need support.

The bonus of a good child ball is that you will feel proud and loved and successful as a parent.

BALL FIVE: WORK/CAREER

There are many reasons people work — to earn money, to contribute to society, to improve their lives or the lives of those around them, or to make the world better. I spend around 2000 hours each year working. I love it. I would even do my job if I didn't get paid. Speaking to and empowering women fills my heart with joy. They say if you find a job you love you will never work another day in your life — and that is certainly true for me.

Not having a job doesn't mean you don't have an active work ball. Working on your work ball is very important — given that we all need money and a purpose to live! If you are currently unemployed, then act as if you have a job — get up and be ready to start the day at 9 a.m. and spend all day researching jobs, learning new skills or doing anything that will get you closer to your goal of your dream role.

Some of you may not need a 'job'. You may not need to work, but you still need a purpose. Whether your purpose is to support others in charity work or to look pretty and go to lunch, be sure of what your purpose actually is.

One of my favourite TV programmes was the New Zealand series *Outrageous Fortune*. In one episode, two of the best characters, Munter and Van, were sitting on the bonnet of their car looking for a job in the newspaper. Van asks Munter 'What's a career?' and Munter replies 'I think it's like a job but it's bigger!'

I guess that's fairly accurate. Some people have jobs — a place where they work doing whatever suits them at the time, for money — and some people have careers. Career people tend to have a plan. They have chosen a specific area that they want to work in and they progress through that field. Many women take jobs just to bring income into the family without ever allowing themselves to think about a career.

ASK YOURSELF:
- Do I have a job or a career?
- How is work for me at the moment? Is it stressful, busy or hard? Or is it boring and unfulfilling?
- What's going on at work at the moment? What do I need to keep my eye on?
- What is important? Who is important?

- Maybe I don't have a job I love — what can I do to change this? More training? Apply for a new role? Do some self-development? Learn a new skill?

I remember when I was in my twenties being told that I couldn't have a career *and* a family. Even in the 1980s there was still some limited thinking around, that you had to choose. I remember thinking 'I will do what I want', and that having both must be possible.

I had seen 'career women' around who had the benefit of a career and a family. I wanted to be a dressed-up woman in a power suit holding a baby.

And then it happened. I got pregnant with my first child. I was so excited and completely immersed in all things baby. Then once my son arrived I decided that I was never going to leave the house without him. I was totally besotted. Leaving him to go to the letterbox seemed like a bad idea.

For three months I sat staring at this heavenly creature that I had created. I spent all my time learning how to be the perfect mother. I read books and did courses and I loved it.

When Oscar was three months old, a friend approached me to help with a new fashion brand he was working on. I gave him a few ideas and found I really enjoyed being asked for my opinion on something that I knew so much about. It was a welcome contrast to not knowing what I was doing with my new little human project!

The fashion project that started as helping a friend turned into a seven-year contract as an art director. It was an amazing job. I was working with cool people. I was being creative and I was in charge of stuff I knew — fashion and people. The work was a series of short contracts so I wasn't working full-time, but when it was on it was on.

Oscar travelled with me the whole time and loved it. Over the next three years two more babies arrived and I just carried on. Each baby travelled with me for the first year — the models and crew were great babysitters.

People were quick to judge about the amount of time I was away and to question what I was doing working and travelling with such a young family. But I loved it. I liked having some other focus than family. I liked being good at something — something that I knew I could control! I had a creative outlet — I spent time with amazing people and we travelled to some amazing places. It was never really my plan, but it worked out.

Because I have always been more of a 'hell yeah' girl than a 'yeah nah' one, I gave it a crack. It was one of the best jobs I have ever had.

People said that I was lucky to have so much support — but I don't believe in lucky. My husband and I chose to stay in the small town we grew up in because we wanted our children to have a close relationship with our parents, their grandparents. We planned that. Having four grandparents up the road is a huge bonus to the working parents of four children! My children have fantastic memories of those days at Grandma's and all have brilliant relationships with all of their grandparents.

So is it reasonable to work full-time with four young children? I think yes, as long as everyone is happy and cared for. The bonus of contract work meant that I had blocks of time when I was at home to be 100 per cent mummy and then blocks of time when I was away. It was a massive juggle, but I don't think it was as exhausting as it is for parents who work full-time all the time. Contract work gave me the flexibility and variety that I needed.

Support and planning were the keys: having the right support in place and planning *everything*. I made all the meals one day ahead so that we never got to 5 p.m. wondering what was for dinner. I had the week's activities and all the gear required for three children under four laid out in the lounge. I had lists everywhere.

I decided that I needed more structured help as the children got older, so I employed a gorgeous woman called Melissa. She had an incredible passion for children and loads of early childhood teaching experience. The kids loved her. Like a special aunty who came each day, Melissa took them on adventures, dropped them at kindy and made them snacks.

When Oscar was five years old, he came home from playing with his friend Geordie and asked me 'Who is Geordie's Melissa?' I said that Geordie didn't have a Melissa. Oscar said, 'Why not? Who looks after him?' I told him that Geordie's mum looked after him and Oscar said, 'That's weird, eh?'

Children always think that whatever is happening in their home is normal. If Mum works then that's normal, if you have a 'Melissa' then that's normal.

So many working parents get hung up on making things 'normal', but happy is way better than normal. If you are a happy mum who loves what you do and you have the right support in place, it will all work. Unsupported, unhappy people make the worst parents. No one is winning when everyone is grumpy. After a while I got grumpy. I was exhausted. My children were five, three and one and I decided that I needed a break. I needed to play with some

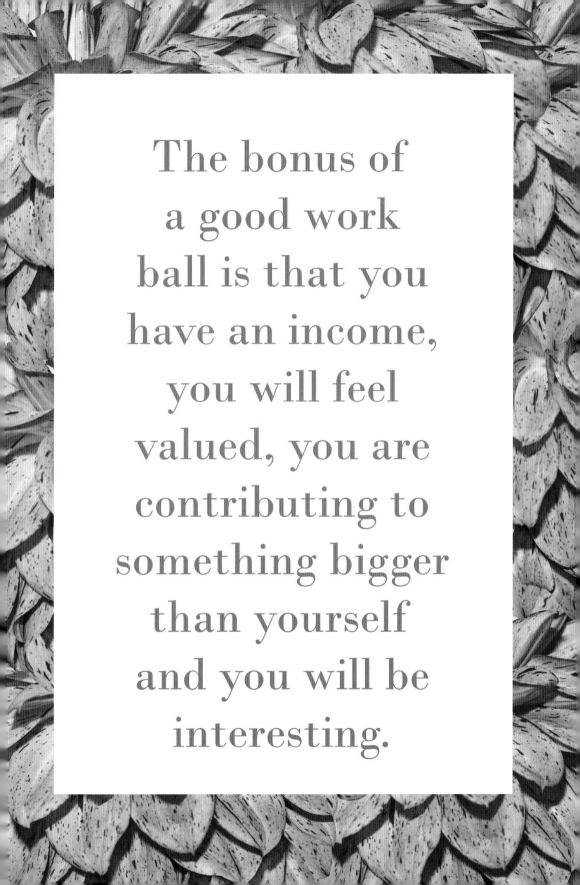

The bonus of
a good work
ball is that you
have an income,
you will feel
valued, you are
contributing to
something bigger
than yourself
and you will be
interesting.

playdough. I wanted to go to the park. So I quit. I put down the work ball and played. It was awesome. And then I was off onto my next thing!

Women work for many reasons. Some for money, as having two incomes is no longer a bonus but a necessity for so many families. Some women work for passion — they love their job and love doing it. Some work just to get out of the house! (When Oscar was a baby I used to help out at a fashion boutique. I loved it. I was never there for more than three hours, covering the busy periods, but I got all dressed up and left the house. I looked good, I smelt good. That wasn't always easy to do when I was at home!)

ASK YOURSELF:

- What is it that I would really like to do?
- What am I good at?
- Whose job do I want?

Life is actually quite long. We are living longer and working longer than we ever have. Just because you have turned 40, don't think that it is too late to change careers. Many of us will work until we are 70 . . . what do you want to do for the next 30 years?

BALL SIX: THE PARENT/ FAMILY BALL

Some people never see their family. Others see them every day. Regardless of which way your life works, your parents gave you life and deserve some attention.

Too bad if they are annoying. You used to annoy them! Find something that you have in common. Take them to the movies, the garden centre — get them to join in your life. Invite them places. Love them. One day they will be gone.

This ball may be an extended family ball. You may not still have your parents but you may spend lots of time with siblings, cousins, aunts . . .

Harry Chapin's famous song 'Cat's in the Cradle' is a great story of how our priorities change throughout life. When we are young our parents are 'busy' struggling to find time to spend with us, then when we grown up we are 'busy' struggling to find time to spend with our parents!

When you have a parent with health issues or problems that need a lot of time and attention, make sure you are getting support. It can be physically and mentally exhausting being a caregiver or support person.

At a workshop I ran in Christchurch a woman mentioned how exhausting it was supporting her mother who was living with dementia. Another woman sitting at the table was also caring for her elderly mum. They swapped stories over lunch and now meet weekly for lunch to share their stories. Finding someone who understands what you are dealing with can make a huge difference in feeling supported.

ASK YOURSELF:
- What do my parents need from me?
- What do my parents want from me? Maybe I need to visit, maybe I need to phone them.
- What help/support do I have?

As people age, often their world gets smaller. They have less going on and they lose their ability to cope with a lot of things. Don't overload them. Make regular plans to visit or call. Don't let them down. You phoning them might be just one of 18 things you are doing that day, but for them it might be the only thing they have to look forward to. You may be busy leading a huge life but they might be at home alone, waiting to hear from you.

They love you. They are proud of you. They want to hear little stories about your life. They want to be involved.

Unless they don't! Maybe you don't get on with your parents. Maybe you have no relationship at all. Make sure you are happy with this situation. Life can be very short and there is nothing as painful as regret. Time is a great healer and it is never too late to reconnect. You don't have to like everything about each other, but you can still be part of each other's lives.

Your children will watch how you treat your parents — what are they learning from you about how to treat you in your old age?

I don't think that we give old people the respect they deserve. Yes they can be frustrating and small-minded and difficult, but they can also be wise and interesting and wonderful. Like any relationship, if you focus on what is great about them and what you enjoy it will make your time together more fun.

The same goes for siblings. How long has it been since you caught up with your brother or sister?

When we live busy lives we can easily go several years without seeing people who are important to us. Social media is a great way of keeping track of cousins', nieces' and nephews' lives. Just make sure you add some real contact in there every now and then!

ASK YOURSELF:
- Who could I connect with?
- Who needs me right now?

The bonus of
a good parent
or family ball
is that you will
feel connected,
compassionate
and supportive.

BALL SEVEN: BEING A FRIEND

Friends are important. Having good friends is vital to a happy life. People without friends do not live as long as people with great friendship connections.

When I say friends, I am talking about good friends. Not Facebook friends. Real people who add value to your life. People who fill your heart with joy when you see them — not the ones who make you cringe when their name comes up on your phone.

As we grow and change, the people we spend time with also changes. It's OK to let go of friendships that no longer serve you. It is part of your growth. As you grow, sometimes you grow apart from people. Your values and interests change.

ASK YOURSELF:
- If I won a free fancy dinner and was only allowed to take three people (who were not related to me), who would I choose?
- Who would I add if I was allowed to take five people?

Being a good friend takes work. It takes effort. A true friend has a sincere interest in your life.

I think that good friendship is a little like tennis — you need a good load of balls bouncing back and forth. One-way friendships can lead to resentment if you are always the person doing all the 'work'. If you are constantly the person phoning, organising, inviting and visiting, it can feel very one-sided.

Be open and honest with your friends — tell them when you have a lot on your plate so they will understand that you may not be as available as you usually are. Let them know if you need their support. People are not mind-readers, and like any relationship it is important that you express what you need to ensure that you feel loved and supported.

Make sure your friends know that they are important to you. Thanking them and telling them how much they mean to you is a great way to honour your friendship.

I have a very diverse group of friends — childhood friends, business friends, spiritual friends, parenting friends, funny friends, clever friends — friends who share different touch points in my life. Many women worry about their friends not liking each other — this is not your problem. You only need to be responsible for the relationship you have with your friends. Don't get tied up in what other people think of your people!

ASK YOURSELF:

- Who are my friends?
- What's going on for them right now?
- When was the last time we caught up?

Make sure you keep note of birthdays, anniversaries and things that are important to them.

If you have a friend who needs special care and attention, then they may need their own ball! Friends who are dealing with big stuff need lots of support. Be honest about what you can do for them. Letting a friend down in their time of need will make a large dent in your friendship.

It is worth having a friend audit every now and then to make sure that you are spending time with the people you care about the most. When you have a good look at your list of friends, you may find that some of them add no value to your life. Some you don't even enjoy the company of anymore. I think that it is vital that you put your time and effort into those who add value to your life.

Some 'friends' are merely life lint — like the lint you find in your pocket, adding no value but taking up space. You don't even know where these people came from, but somehow they ended up in your life! Set these 'friends' free. This sounds a bit ruthless, but you simply do not have time to have your day, your calendar and your contact list bogged down with people who don't actually float your boat! Your life will improve, as you will have more time to spend with those who you truly love rather than keeping lint happy. Live a lint-free life!

Take the time you have been spending with these lint friends and go out in search of new and interesting people. When in the market for a new friend, it pays to think about the type of friend that you want. Do you want a creative friend to share ideas with? Do you want a gym buddy to exercise with? Tell people that you are in the market for some new friends. They might be able to recommend people or introduce you to some of theirs.

When I talk to women about their friendships, they are often embarrassed to admit that they do not have many friends or that they want more. Feeling unpopular and unworthy of good friends usually goes right back to childhood, when you first felt 'not good enough'.

ASK YOURSELF:

- Did I have a lot of friends as a child?
- Have I been treated badly by friends in the past?
- What beliefs do I have about friendships as an adult?

As adults many people find creating new friendships difficult. They are not sure how to get new friends.

For a start, you need to go places and meet people. Some people you meet you will feel a real connection with — when this happens, make a move. Ask them out! Ask if they want to go to the movies or meet for lunch. Suggest doing something together.

Some people have a huge number of friends, some only have one. There is no right number — it's just about whatever you feel happy with. If you feel like you would like some new friends, then go and hunt some down. If your friendship card feels full, then get busy honouring the friends you have.

The bonus of
a good friend
ball is that you
will have fun
and support
and love.

The hobby ball
is something
that we tend to
put down when
other balls get
big and busy.

BALL EIGHT: THE HOBBY BALL

Do you have a hobby? Do you spend all weekend following a sport or collecting honey or breeding cats? Maybe you are on a committee? Your hobby might be community service or volunteering for a cause.

Unfortunately, many women give up on their hobbies and interests as they dedicate time and money to their busy families

Hobbies take time and money and effort. The effort part is easy because you are usually so filled with passion for your hobby that it is your joy.

I have so many hobbies. I love 'nana things' (as my husband calls them) like embroidery, knitting, sewing and scrapbooking. I have always been keen on creative pastimes and love to make anything. Luckily for me my daughters both love to dance, so making dance costumes for them ticks both my creativity and good mother boxes! I have boxes of fabric and tins of beads and buttons waiting to be made into something.

But for now my hobby ball is on hold. With four children and a busy career I simply do not have time to be making things — at the moment. My hobby time will come.

I feel lucky to know what I love and to have so many things that I am interested in. Many women are not interested in much. They have lost touch with the things that they enjoy.

Having an interest or a hobby can get you out and meeting new people. So, what are you interested in? What did you love as a child?

When I was little I wanted to be a florist. I still want to be a florist! Flower arranging is something I plan to do one day. The things that we loved as children are often still things we love as adults — it's just that in the busy-ness of life we have forgotten about these interests. Having interests makes you interesting.

What is interesting about you? Make an 'interesting' list. If there is nothing on your list, then you aren't interesting!

Spend time on things that interest you. It doesn't matter if they interest anyone else. Your interests will lead you down interesting paths. With the amount of information we can now access on the internet, there is nothing that you cannot learn about these days.

Pets and animals play a big part in some people's lives. Do you have fur babies? Are you a mad cat woman? I adore my cats and love hanging out with them. Pets can be time-consuming and expensive — but also very rewarding. The unconditional love, companionship and fun you can add to your life by being a pet owner is wonderful. Being of service can also be a hobby. Volunteering, supporting and helping charities can be very rewarding and teach you new skills. Where can you add value? If you are good at something, maybe you can help others by offering your experience and time. Coaching, teaching and contributing to your community will get you out and about and connected to others.

ASK YOURSELF:
- What do I want to learn?
- What courses or events do I want to attend?
- Do I need to buy equipment or supplies for my hobby?

Find three hobbies that you love: one to make you money, one to keep you in shape and one to be creative.

— unknown

BALL NINE: YOUR ENVIRONMENT

This is about where you live. Do you have a large property? Does this take up a lot of your time? Are you renovating or redecorating? Are you moving?

Moving house or renovating can be a crazy time, when this ball seems to take over everything. When your environment is in chaos, everything else seems to follow. We renovated recently and it was crazy: no laundry or kitchen for six weeks, tradespeople everywhere and what felt like 300 decisions to make every single day!

Living in an environment that you love will make you feel good. Filling your home with things that you love will add joy to your life.

I don't have anything in my home that doesn't make me feel good. Ugly things make me anxious and I feel physically uncomfortable when surrounded by things I don't like.

I have never been good at housework. In fact, I hate it. I am no good at it and I don't enjoy it. I would rather work and pay someone to do it for me. I can spend hours arranging vases and paintings but have no interest in dusting and vacuuming!

Some people seemed owned by their homes. They spend so much time on them — the constant gardening, sweeping, cleaning and tidying. This is a great thing if you love it and get immense satisfaction out of it, but what if all the upkeep of your environment is stopping you from doing the things that you really love? The things that are important to you?

Many women feel obligated to be amazing homemakers — constantly apologising for the state of their environments. I do not judge people on the state of their houses and cars — in fact, I find messy people are usually more interesting than people with immaculate environments.

If you are spending lots of time making your home perfect for yourself, then good for you. If you are just doing it for the approval of others, then stop right now. Life is too short to have a dull life and a perfect home.

I have always been messy. I have so much going on and so much that I want to do that living in a tidy space has never been a huge priority. However, I have noticed that my body responds positively to a bit of order, and spending time keeping spaces tidy actually helps me feel good and perform better. Simple things like making the bed and putting clothes away are still daily challenges for me, but they do make me feel good.

I have spent a lot of time studying feng shui and love the idea of harmonious energy flowing through my home. I remember when the children were very young and two of them would not stay in bed. I was reading a feng shui book that talked about the direction of the head of the bed. I moved their beds and their sleeping patterns changed. Amazing. And free!

As energetic beings, the energy flow in our homes makes a huge difference to the quality of our lives. Using simple techniques to clear the energy in our homes is as important as clearing the dust.

Getting rid of things that no longer serve you will add a lot of energy to your home. Decluttering is something I am constantly doing. With four children who are constantly changing, there is always something to get rid of!

My favourite technique is to remove everything from a room and to only put back what I love. Anything else I get rid of. Your trash will be another person's treasure. Move on and allow new things to enter your home.

Marie Kondo's book *The Life-Changing Magic of Tidying Up* is a great place to start to help you to decide what you need and do not need in your home.

In my time as a wardrobe stylist I spent hours in over-cluttered wardrobes with women telling me stories about why they were keeping their clothes. Fifty per cent of the clothes in most women's wardrobes do not fit them and 25 per cent of the things that we have hanging up we don't even like! You are better to have 10 things in your wardrobe that you love and that love you back by fitting you and suiting your body shape than having an overstuffed wardrobe of things that will never work.

ASK YOURSELF:
- How much time do I spend on my home environment?
- What do I need to focus on at home?
- What improvements at home would dramatically improve my life?

Your home
should tell the
story of your life
and be a
collection of
what you love.

— Nate Berkus

BALL TEN: YOUR SPIRITUAL BALL

I have a huge faith — a faith in god, the universe, mother earth, spirit — whatever you want to call it. Faith is the foundation of all self-love. Believing in something has helped me learn to trust — trust the universe, trust god . . .

Who is your god? Work out what you believe in — not what your grandma believed or what you were told to believe, but what you believe.

I had a very strange relationship with all things god when I was younger. My father is an atheist and my mother a disillusioned Presbyterian. We didn't attend church, although I do remember going to Sunday school in the early days.

I have always struggled with the idea of sin. Intuitively, I felt that god was my friend; that my kind of god was always there for me. I did not have to visit a certain building or read a certain book for him to hold an interest in me.

The upside of not having a very strong religious base was that I did not have anything to unlearn — I was a blank canvas and have over the past 20 years taken pieces of different practices and belief systems to create a set of beliefs that I love.

Many people subscribe to many different 'spiritual beliefs'. I was once asked my religion at a church-run parenting group. Without thinking, I said, 'I am a freelancer.' That was actually very accurate. Having not being raised in a religious family I never really had a strong 'faith base', and for many years was a little annoyed at the hypocrisy of organised religion. I knew people who claimed to be 'good Christians' and yet behaved appallingly. I have never been a big fan of rules and could not understand the upside of people following something which seemed to me to be pointless.

As part of the self-discovery journey that I started in my late twenties, I started reading some wonderful books by spiritual teachers. I was first introduced to Louise Hay's *You Can Heal Your Life* when I was 18. Louise was the founder of the self-love movement and an incredible metaphysical teacher. She went on to create Hay House — a publishing house which published books by authors like Wayne Dyer, Deepak Chopra, Don Miguel Ruiz, Marianne Williamson, Denise Lynn, Neale Donald Walsch, Doreen Virtue, Sonia Choquette, Cheryl Richardson and Anita Moorjani (see my book list on page 205, which features many of these authors). I have been to many Hay House conferences to hear these people speak and have read so many of their books. These teachers taught me about faith and love and to follow my intuition.

It took me a long time and many, many books before I actually worked out where I sat on the issue of religion. When I read Neale Donald Walsch's *Conversations with God (Book One)* I was relieved to hear that someone else had queries similar to mine and was grateful that he had asked the questions during his 'conversation'.

I believe that in order to lead a powerful life you need to be connected to a spiritual power. My personal power comes from my ability to trust in the universe and in my god.

Dr Robert Holden, author of *Be Happy* and *Authentic Success*, taught me the importance of having a daily spiritual practice. For some people a daily spiritual practice is attending church or saying prayers or reading passages from sacred texts; for others it might be a walk on the beach or listening to music or mediating. Do whatever works for you.

I think that if everyone could agree that there are many gods and forms of religion, then the world would be a happier and calmer place. Each to their own. Back your own horse. Believe in whatever gets you through.

ASK YOURSELF:
- What do I believe in?
- What helps me to feel strong?
- Who has similar beliefs to me?
- What could I do to get in touch with my personal power?

Connecting
to something
bigger than
yourself is a
great way to
feel supported
in your life.

So, now that you have identified your balls, think about what you currently have in the air: proactive ball care is what being a good juggler is all about!

- Which balls are going well?
- Which balls are you close to dropping?
- Which balls do you want to drop?

Rank your balls from 1 to 10 in order of importance for you right now. How do you really feel? Are you tired? Are you bored?

- If you want to feel loved — focus on your partner, child or friend balls.
- If you want to feel successful — focus on your work, child or hobby balls.
- If you want to feel supported — focus on your parent, family and friends balls.
- If you want to feel connected — focus on your child, partner or spiritual balls.
- If you want to feel energetic — focus on your health or environment balls.
- If you want to feel creative — focus on your environment or hobby balls.

CHAPTER THREE

Purpose and priorities

Cast your mind back . . . can you remember when life was all about you? What *you* were going to do at the weekend, what *you* were going to wear on Saturday night, where *you* were going to go for New Year's Eve . . .

When I was 20 years old my life was so simple. It was all about me! I was working, Mark and I were skipping through life, planning holidays and going to concerts, and everything was very easy. It was just me, my boyfriend and my job. Life is easy when you only have three balls in the air.

And then we decided to get married. (Well I decided, but Mark still thinks it was his idea!). I quickly developed a wedding ball! It was big and very exciting. For six months it was the only ball I was interested in. After the wedding it was a relief to go back to just three balls.

And then I got pregnant. After reading many books and thinking that getting pregnant could take up to 12 months, approximately four weeks after I came off the pill I was done. Up the duff. And very, very excited!

My 'baby ball' got big very quickly. I read and planned and painted and shopped. Project baby was the only ball I was interested in.

And then it happened. I became a mother. Holy shit!

It was incredible. Never before had I been so consumed by something, 24/7. I can remember thinking how amazing being a mother was. I told my own mother she had no idea what I was going through! I had grown a person. I was now feeding a person. This person was perfect. There was nothing else that mattered! For weeks I didn't juggle a thing. I just sat with this perfect ball on my lap.

When Oscar was four months old I started a new job. It was very exciting. And so the juggle began.

Eighteen months later, Ruby was born. I had a living doll. She was beautiful and calm. I was happiness-filled.

Two years later I had Tilly. She was like a cherub, cute and round and wise with blonde curls.

Life was a mish-mash of work and kindy and playgroups and birthday parties . . .

And then I quit. I was sick of the juggle. I wanted to be at home playing in a sandpit. I wanted my nanny's job! So I took her job and quit mine.

Within four months I was bored, so I started my own business. I wanted to help women — and Lisa O'Neill Stylist was born. No more children. I was a career woman. I had plans . . .

And then Ruby started school. I was at home with just one baby. I cried. I phoned my husband and told him I needed another one . . . hello, Felix!

DOING IT ALL

Once Felix arrived I realised that I no longer needed to prove myself by being Mrs Wonderful. I didn't need to be on every committee that had a spot. I didn't need to attend every school fund-raiser. I needed to do a good job of keeping my balls up in the air!

I have a busy life, and I like it that way. I have four children, a husband, four parents and in-laws living in my street, I work a lot and I have some wonderful people in my world whom I want to share time with. It takes a lot of planning to juggle so many balls.

I have had to put down my hobby ball for the time being. I love to sew and create and am also keen on being on committees and supporting community groups, but quite honestly I do not have time. These are all things that I have done before and they are things that I will go back to doing again — later, when I have some space!

There will be times in your life when you are trying to integrate a new ball. Perhaps you are going back to work after having a family, maybe you have just met a new partner or are having a third child. This time is critical and you need to make sure that the other balls are prepared.

It is helpful if you can plan for these events. Make some lists!

People ask me how I do it all — and the truth is, I don't. I have it all — just not all on the same day! Some days I am at home juggling the children, other days I am away juggling work. Once you have children you never put down this ball — it is always there. But when I travel for work I am able to keep them in my mind's eye while I focus on my work ball.

Many women try to do everything every day. They cook, clean, work and parent all at the same time. This is a juggling disaster.

Always know what your most important ball is and do not take your eyes off it. Having a solid hour of work time and then a solid hour of time with your child is way better than having two hours in your office trying to work with your child!

Having a plan and having 'the balls' to prioritise your balls is the secret. I call it 'the highest bidder'.

Every day I think about who the highest bidder is. Some days you have a huge work day planned and your child is sick. Highest bidder: your child needs you.

Three of my children have now been diagnosed with Type 1 diabetes.

Three times we have been rushed to hospital for a week with no notice. There is only one ball that matters when you have a child diagnosed with anything. All other balls get put away.

Any parent will tell you that when their kid gets hospitalised the world stops and you get one focus. The hardest bit is when the drama is over and you have to go home and pick up all the balls and start juggling them all together again!

Some days you have planned a dinner party for friends and your mum has a heart attack. Highest bidder. At that moment your dinner party ceases to exist and the only thing that matters is your mum and that ambulance.

So there are times we cannot plan for — but this is not an excuse not to plan. Having a plan is critical to managing a full life. Planning is good — worrying is not.

I refuse to 'pre-worry'. Pre-worry is the thing you do where you think of all the things that could go wrong and why something won't work. Planning will help this. If you have a plan for what you want to do, have considered why you are doing it and have considered where the potential risks, are then there is nothing more that can be done.

Say you have a kid's birthday party to plan. Once you have decided what, where and how you are going to do it, the only thing left is to get what is on the list and get on with it. Worrying about the party will not change it. Good planning will.

We all know that when you are dealing with children (or in fact any humans), there is only so much you can plan. Stuff will go wrong. Plans change.

Learn to bounce, not break, when things go wrong.

DIS-EASE

A good juggler is agile, flexible and calm. If you are scrambled and unplanned you will not be able to focus on keeping your balls in the air.

I see this all the time. In the thousands of women that I have met and worked with over the past 20 years, I see similar themes. Many are scrambled. They are dashing from one thing to another, feeling like a failure in every area of their lives. They are worried that they are under-parenting, underperforming at work, not supporting their partner and haven't spoken to their friends for weeks, let alone found time to get their hair cut!

I meet hundreds of women who are all suffering from the same dis-ease — not a disease like a medical issue, but living in a constant state of dis-ease. Nothing is easy. Life is very hard.

Do either of the following states sound familiar?

Mental chaos

It's often all too much. You forget appointments, can't remember what time you need to be where, are constantly apologising and catching up. Dashing from work to home and back to work, you become no good to anyone as you are simply so scattered that you have turned into human confetti. Your energy is everywhere. I know how this feels! You wake up exhausted and your heart is already racing. Dr Libby Weaver calls it 'Rushing Woman's Syndrome' . . . dashing from here to there, living on a cocktail of coffee, adrenaline and wine. You kick-start your body with coffee, dash about, then arrive home ready to start the chaos of the evening and grab a wine to wind down. This can work for a short while, but if done over a long period, this life becomes addictive and you will trash your body and your mind. If you feel like you never get your list 'done' and you are constantly apologising, you may be in this state! You need time, space and sleep. Clear some stuff off the calendar.

You need time,
space and sleep.
Clear some stuff
off the calendar.

The great pretender

These women are perfect — or at least that's what they want you
to believe. They have perfect children, perfect homes and perfect
husbands. Bullshit! They are as see-through as plastic wrap. They
think they are fooling people but they are only fooling themselves.
They have no idea what they want or how to get it. They are
following a formula that says if they collect enough things and
make everything right, then life must be good — right? Wrong.
They are like hollow Easter eggs: all shiny and well decorated but
with nothing inside. They have been brought up on a diet of other
people's ideas and do not really know what makes them tick. They
aren't sure what they believe or what they stand for. They feel
disconnected from their own lives but cannot admit it to anyone.

PLAN, PLAN AND PLAN SOME MORE

The greatest gift my work has given me is travel. When you travel, you have to plan. You need to be on time. (This is a hard one for me!) When I travel, I have to plan what I am going to wear, what I am going to do, who I am going to see and where I am going to be. A bit of planning goes a long way, and can be the water for your chaos fire.

When I plan, I work backwards. I write down what I have on in the evening, then go backwards through the day.

For example, if I have an event at 7 p.m., I need to be at the venue at 6 p.m., which means I have to get dressed at 5 p.m., which means I have to eat at 4 p.m., and so on. Factoring in time to eat, travel and get ready is one bit that I used to leave out. Not smart! I can spend four hours a day travelling, eating and getting dressed! It's no wonder that I was always out of time.

I write down whatever I have locked in for the day: events, appointments. I then ask myself two very important questions:

1. What else do I *want* to do that day?

2. What else do I *have* to do that day?

THE WANTS

In the chaos of our lives it is super-duper easy to stop doing stuff that you want to do. It becomes a bit hard, a bit frivolous and quite simply you don't have enough time. Something has to give, right? Wrong. Stopping doing the things that you want to is a sure-fire way to guarantee that you will turn into a bitter old bitch, grumping and moaning about your life.

No one wants a bitter old bitch as a mother, a friend or a wife. For the protection of yourself and your relationships, I urge you to make things that you want to do a priority.

At my workshops, I ask women what they love to do. What makes them happy. I ask them to write a list. Then I ask them to write down the last time that they did any of those things . . .

One woman told me her biggest passion was skiing. I asked her when she had last gone skiing and it was nine years earlier!

Now, I get that skiing is not something you can pop off and do in your lunch break, but my point is that you need to prioritise your happiness. You need to fill your heart with joy so you can sail through this thing called life with a smile on your face!

Make a list now of all the things that you love to do. Now plan to do them.

THE HAVE-TOS

What do you *have* to do? Dentist appointment? School concert? Work meeting? By putting your have-tos into your day plan you can then see how much time you have left for your love-tos. Before a have-to gets written down, make sure it really is vital.

ASK YOURSELF:
- Can someone else do it?
- What will happen if I don't do it?

Getting a balance of want-tos and have-tos is the secret to having a balanced life and a sane mind. When we do things that we want to, it shows on our faces. We are happy — our energy increases. Only doing things that you 'have to' will drag you down and make you a resentful, grumpy person.

I also have monthly lists for birthdays and important dates to remember. If you load these into your phone, you will never forget another one. I also have term lists with the priorities for each term — drama productions, dance exams, school trips.

Creating a calendar of the whole year with a list of you have planned is a good idea. I find it helps me plan my work, my travel and my time at home.

Grab a piece of paper and list the next 12 months on it. Write down everything that you know you have on each month: important birthdays, school holidays, travel, public holidays, etc.

Now you can add in some fun stuff. After any period of great busy-ness, I lock in a weekend treat for myself. I need to plan to refill my tank!

THE PURPOSE PLANNER

I love planning. I also love stationery, and so I have created the Purpose Planner. This is a copy of all the systems that I have created to keep my life flowing and heading in the right direction.

I found that when looking for tools to help me manage my big juggle, I could never find the right one. I found 'corporate diaries' that started at 8 a.m. and went to 6 p.m. I found 'family planning diaries' that included grocery lists but had no place for me to record my meetings. So I started making day sheets that listed my priorities for the day: the things I needed to do, buy and cook, and the people I needed to phone and meet.

Every Friday I have a meeting with myself. I go over the next week's events and list anything that needs to be organised, provided, bought or arranged. I write lists and notes of people, events, priorities, birthdays. Meetings with Self are vital for any good juggler. You cannot juggle successfully if you do not know how many balls you have in the air, and their status. I love my calendar on my phone and have many digital tools that I use to remind me and prompt me and support my schedule but I still find that sitting with a pad of paper and a pen helps my brain. It helps me to nut out how things are going to work best. I also write up a weekly plan to stick on the fridge. This allows me to physically see that week and where any congested parts are.

I strongly suggest you make your meeting official. Go to a local café or set yourself up at a table with a coffee, a nice pen and your chosen stationery.

Write down everything that everyone in your household has on that week. I go through a checklist of all six people in our house and what their needs are for the week. Sometimes children need time, sometimes they need money, sometimes they need physical help. Some weeks they need all of these things!

Now block out time for your priorities. If your priority is health and fitness, make sure your diary shows that, with your exercise sessions blocked out. If your priority is one of your children, block out time for them.

In my meeting I also like to plan meals, red-flagging difficult evenings when everyone is out and about. Having four children was so much easier when they were little and all went to the same places! Now we have six individuals in the house — and six different sets of transport, gear and support are needed!

On a Sunday night I have a debrief meeting with the family — nothing too formal, just a run-through of what everyone has on for the week ahead. I brief them on my work priorities for the week, who is doing what, and ask all of them what they need from me and Mark. (I think it is important to teach children to think about what they need and to be able to ask for any assistance. I have found as they have grown older, what I think they need and what they actually need are quite different things!)

Once you have a clear plan of what is going on, who needs what, and when things are happening, you can smooth out any bumps. You can also see where you might need some help.

Instead of stressing about a potential issue, try to turn your mind into wonder mode. I wonder who could pick Felix up for me? I wonder who might be able to drop off this parcel? Go to wonder before you go to panic.

ASK YOURSELF:
- What do I have to do?
- What do I need to do?
- What do I want to do?
- Who can help?

LIGHTENING THE LOAD

When you are juggling so many balls there will be times when you will want or need to throw one to someone else.

My advice is to get rid of as many balls as you possibly can. I used to admire people who did everything. Now I admire people who ask for help!

Have a look at your roles (see page 14). Make a list of all the things that you do in each of those roles. Now get a highligh ter and run it through all the things that you don't like doing.

Once you have found the things that you definitely do not like to do, start to brainstorm with yourself as to who else might do them.

For example, a friend of mine who is a single parent of two school-aged children really hates making school lunches. Every day it was her first thought on waking: how much she hated those lunchboxes and the challenge of filling them with things that were healthy, fun and would actually get eaten.

Her daughter kept talking about her friend's lunches — she always had the best lunches, apparently. One morning the two mothers met. My friend congratulated the other mother on her famous lunches, saying that preparing lunches was a constant problem in her morning. The lunchbox mother said she loved making lunches, and was planning to write a book of lunch ideas for busy mums. She needed to earn some money to fulfill her dream of writing her lunchbox book, so my friend offered to pay her to make her two children's lunches. Boom — everyone was happy!

I love this story as it illustrates how some problems can be so easily solved.

I hate housework. I always have. I just feel there are so many other things that I want to do with my time. My mother-in-law, however, is famous for her knowledge of cleaning products and for owning a home so clean that you could eat off the base of the shower.

She was telling me once over a coffee that she hated cooking. She could never think of what to cook and she never enjoyed it. So I offered to cook meals for her. She came to my place and while she cleaned, I cooked. She left with three meals and I had a clean house. Perfect!

Find some people to throw some of your balls to. Give people the opportunity to give. It is part of the human condition that most of us like to help others. It makes us feel good.

ASK YOURSELF:

- Who can I ask for help?
- Who do I ask for help?
- Who do I rely on?
- Who are the people that I always ask for help?
- Who is my backstop?

It is worth mentioning here the importance of looking after your support people. If it's your sister or mother or a friend who always has the kids or gets you out of a hole, make sure that you value them. Show them that you are grateful. Buy them a gift, write them a card. Yes, they might be the kids' grandmother or aunty, but they still deserve to feel honoured and not taken for granted.

Never neglect good catchers!

Another great catcher might be your partner. If they are truly invested in your wellbeing, they will be there for you. They will support you.

I have been fortunate to hear author Neale Donald Walsch speak on a couple of occasions. He is a brilliant teacher and speaker and delivers wonderful messages. His book, *Conversations with God*, is one of my all-time favourites (see page 205 for my best-ever book list).

At one session, Neale asked us all to go home and thank our partner for witnessing our lives. At first I thought that was kind of odd. But the more I thought about it, the more I liked it.

Some people literally have no one witnessing their lives. No one knows whether or not they get out of bed, whether they have a good or a bad day. I remember reading a newspaper article about a man who had died and no one had noticed for four months. No one was witnessing him.

Someone who listens to your stories, who goes places with you and who knows what you do is a witness. Maybe you don't have a partner — but hopefully you all have a few witnesses. Thank them. The witnesses in our lives add more value than we realise. Be grateful to your witnesses — they will most likely be one of your ball-catchers.

COMMUNICATION AND CALM

Communicating what's going on in your life to those around you is a great way to improve everyone's understanding. For example, I sat my kids down and explained that I was writing another book and that I was going to need some blocks of uninterrupted time in order to get that done. It is easier if they know that in advance and have some understanding of why, rather than wondering why Mum is working all the time and having no idea what she's doing. Tell your friends that you have a big work project on, or that your son's soccer season is about to start and as the coach you won't have much time free over the next few weeks.

Communicating
what's going on
in your life to
those around you
is a great way to
improve everyone's
understanding.

Planning and
communication
will fix most
problems before
they start.

TIME OUT

Time is my most precious commodity. I was saying to my mum the other night that it would be awesome to be able to phone up and get a time overdraft, like you can get a financial one from your bank. Imagine phoning up your bank manager and asking for an extension on your day! 'Could I just have five more hours this week, please?' That would be handy! Sadly, it is not available. So we need to treat our time with the preciousness that it deserves.

It is very easy to fall under the spell of busy. But often we get so busy being busy that we don't even know what we are busy doing. We only know that our mouth feels dry, our heart is pounding and we want to cancel everything. And sometimes that is exactly what you need to do.

Years ago, when I was running around being a headless chicken — I had four children, meetings to get to, work deadlines, after-school activities, food to cook, blah blah blah — I was complaining to my friend Lesley that I didn't know what to do. She said, 'Just don't do any of it.' I nearly dropped the phone! What did she mean *don't do any of it?* She said it again. She said, 'Just stop. No one will die. You can carry on tomorrow.' I felt a wave of calm wash over me.

Imagine someone giving you permission to stop. To cancel everything. That's what Lesley did. She gave me the permission that I was unable to give myself.

Nowadays, one of the other big benefits of travelling a lot for work is that I get a lot of time alone. This is good for my head.

And this is something I want to encourage all women to get: alone time for your head.

Whether it is a morning walk, an evening mediation or a weekend away — give yourself the gift of alone time. It is very hard to know how you feel or what you think when surrounded by constant activity and noise.

WISE ADVICE

I would like to suggest here that you go out and find a friend who is older than yourself. In the past, women worked together in villages. They shared their knowledge and wisdom was handed down from woman to woman. In the silly, disconnected world we live in today, we miss out on that.

We might get advice from our mothers, but sometimes the gap between us is just too wide. They do not really understand your current situation. Life is moving and changing at such an incredible pace that the gaps between generations are getting much bigger.

Older friends offer such good advice. Wise advice comes from wise people, and in my experience wise people are the ones who have been around the block a couple more times than you have.

Friends with children a couple of stages ahead of yours; friends who will say 'I remember going through that' when you are facing a work, parenting or marriage crisis . . . Their advice might not be any good, but it certainly helps to hang out with someone who has survived whatever your current drama is.

Life can often feel like one continuous drama — bouncing from one phase to another — and it's always nice to have some good company!

Older friends offer such good advice.

LIVING ON PURPOSE

Life has become very 'unsimple'. We rush through busy days, constantly attached to devices, don't concentrate, spend very little time thinking or planning, and as a result generally feel that we are not achieving much. We are in fact achieving a lot, but unfortunately doing a lot badly.

Mindfulness and simplicity have become the new vogue — everyone is telling us to slow down, to have a digital detox and to reduce what we are doing. Mindfulness is just the opposite of mindlessness, which is how most of us go through life! We do things without being fully engaged, just going through the motions.

I have spent time studying mindfulness and love the idea of being fully present and focused, but I struggle with actually being mindful — doing one thing at a time gets boring. I have spent years as a multitasker and I find trying to focus 100 per cent on just one thing is actually quite odd.

I tried it one day when I took my daughter to gymnastics. Instead of sitting chatting to the other mothers, playing on my phone and eating something, I decided to be fully mindful. I was going to give 100 per cent of my attention to Tilly and what she was doing at gym.

About 15 minutes into the session, Tilly came up to me and said, 'What are you doing? You are being really odd!' I laughed and told her that I had decided to be mindful and to give her 100 per cent of my attention. She told me it was creepy and to stop it!

I have created my own solution to stop my attention being so scattered. It is called 'living on purpose'. We can achieve so much if we are purposeful about what we are doing, what we want to achieve and why we are here.

People who live on purpose know what they are doing, why they are doing it, where they are going and what they are in charge of. The definition of purpose is 'the reason for which something exists'. So what is your reason? Why are you here?

I believe that all of us have a big 'why'. Our big purpose. So why do you think you have been given a space in the world? What have you got to contribute? What is your 'why'?

I consider myself incredibly lucky to have worked out my 'why' early. I was very driven from an early age into the world of self-development. I loved it. For the past 20 years I have read, attended workshops, studied information, stretched my thinking and studied every nook and cranny of my life. This did not come from a place of lack — I was not bettering myself, I was actually discovering myself. With each layer I removed, more of me started to appear. Like a human Pass the Parcel, layer by layer I started to see more of who I was and what I had to offer the world.

Empowering people is my 'why'. I am here to empower people to be themselves. Not necessarily to change themselves, but to be *more* of themselves.

Many people go on a journey of self-discovery. They tell me that they are taking six months off to 'find themselves'.

I can understand people wanting some time out, wanting to give themselves some space to develop interests and ideas, but I do not believe that anyone needs to *find* themselves. *You are already here!* What most people need to do is to learn to *like* themselves. To work out what parts of them really are them and which parts are just coatings of bullshit that other people have applied to their lives. Teachers, parents, partners, bosses and siblings can all add coatings — layers of stuff that you believe about yourself that is simply not true.

The more time
you spend getting
to know yourself,
the more you
will like yourself
and the more
you will start
to understand
which bits of you
actually are YOU.

'WHY' CHAPTERS

As we navigate through the different phases of our lives, our purposes change. I don't think that it matters what your purpose is as long as you have one. At certain times of our lives we have different 'why' chapters. These will define your current purpose.

My **'why'** chapters have been:

AGE 0–15: I AM HERE TO LEARN THINGS.
I was a people-pleaser at school. Horribly concerned with what everyone thought of me, I spent huge amounts of energy impressing people who didn't matter. I wanted to be popular, clever, funny and important.

AGE 16–22: I AM HERE TO UNDERSTAND PEOPLE.
I started out in the workplace. I thought I knew everything! I had to learn to understand people — how they worked, what they liked — and to adjust myself accordingly.

AGE 23–28: I AM HERE TO ACHIEVE.
I moved into a family business — which meant that I had to work harder and be better than anyone else to get half as much recognition. I was desperate to succeed and to be successful.

AGE 29–32: I AM HERE TO LOVE.
I became a mother. I learnt the size of love and what it could get you through. I learnt the pure joy of loving so much that I would literally do anything for my children. Everything I did was loaded with love.

AGE 33–39: I AM HERE TO NURTURE.
I learnt the importance of self-care. I nurtured myself. I nurtured those around me. I learnt how to meet the needs of others without neglecting my own. I realised that I had the ability to inspire others. By speaking my truth and sharing my life learnings, I could help others. I became emotionally nutritious!

Working out what is important to you is something that can help when you are stuck on defining your purpose.

- List the things that are super-important to you right now. Is it your children, your career, your partner, your pet . . . ?
- If there was one word that sums up how you want to feel at this point in your life, what is it? Is it successful, free, safe, fun? Choose what you want to be. Pick a word, try it on for a while. See how it fits. You can always change it.

I meet women every day who are wishing and wanting. They want a new career, they want a new man, they want another child. They wish they had studied more, they wish they had lived their life differently.

If you have children, then be an example for them — be someone whom your son would want to marry and someone whom your daughter wants to be like.

The most empowering thing that any woman can do is to live a fabulous life. Living an empowered life is a wonderful way to be an example to those around you. Be inspiring to anyone watching!

Your purpose is
to be the biggest,
grandest and
happiest version
of you that you
can. That is all.

PRIORITIES

When you have a purpose, your priorities become very clear. If your purpose is to be successful, in whatever endeavour, then every day you must plan to do something that brings you along that road. You must stay on track and be aware of the goal.

When planning your time, always keep in the front of your mind what your over-riding purpose is. Your diary should always reflect your priorities and your priorities should tie back to your purpose.

Every now and then I do a little check. I go back through my diary with coloured highlighters (one for each ball) and check what I have been spending my time on. Some months I spend lots of time working, others I spend at home. When I am at home my priority might be to catch up with my husband — he is my priority for that morning or afternoon. Then in the evening I may have dinner with a friend. They are my priority for that evening.

The trick is to make sure that you are covering all your bases, and that you are making yourself a priority in life. Planning in time for yourself is never wasted.

LET GO OF CONTROL

One of the most valuable things that I have learnt is that there is absolutely no point in spending time and energy trying to control things that you cannot control — like people. I used to love to try to control everyone around me. I wanted them to read the books I suggested, watch the movies that I loved, eat the food that I was eating. It didn't work. They simply didn't want to do what I told them!

Control always comes from fear. It packages itself up with a little bit of perfectionism and tells you that if you don't control everything around you, then you will lose the plot. It is like being in a constant tug of war — trying really hard to pull on the rope while you get on with your life. When I was a control freak I was constantly exhausted. Hanging on so tight was just too hard.

The serenity prayer, originally written by American Reinhold Niebuhr, was given to me on a card many years ago. It is a fantastic reminder for me to decide what I can and cannot control. The most commonly quoted version goes:

God grant me the serenity to accept the
things that I cannot change,
The courage to change the things that I can,
And the wisdom to know the difference.

A modern version that I think is funny and quite true goes:

God grant me the serenity to accept the
things that I cannot change,
Coffee to change the things that I can,
And wine to accept the things that I can't.

NOW ASK YOURSELF: CAN I CONTROL THIS?

- No: Good! Don't worry, put it out of your mind.
- Yes: What can I do about it? What am I going to do about it?

When we give up our need to control everyone and everything around us, we gain so much. We learn to trust ourselves. We learn to trust the universe. Trying to predict the outcome of every situation and every person's next move will only make you anxious and stressed.

Trust is the antidote to control. As I learn to trust myself, I learn to trust others and I learn to stop trying to control everything to ensure a 'perfect outcome'.

I think perfectionism is just
fear in fancy shoes and a
mink coat, pretending to be
elegant when actually it's
just terrified. Because there
is nothing underneath that
shiny veneer, perfectionism
is nothing more than a deep
existential angst that says,
again and again "I am not
good enough and I will
never be good enough".

— Elizabeth Gilbert

It took me years to work out that my perfectionism was a symptom of me not ever feeling good enough. I wrote about NGE (Not Good Enough) disease in my first book *Look Gorgeous Be Happy*. So many of us suffer from NGE — in fact, I would go as far as to say that everyone suffers from NGE, just at different levels. Even after years and years of self-discovery and development it can still pop up. New situations, stress and drama can bring you straight out of NGE remission.

Now when I notice myself trying to control something, I ask myself what it is that I feel not good enough about. What has rattled my cage? When we feel out of control we often want to try to control others.

I have a friend who is very passionate about health. She is always researching a new thing, trying new systems to nourish her body. We were talking one day and she was telling me about how well raw food was working for her. She felt amazing, she looked amazing and she had loads of energy. She told me that her only problem was that her husband was not the slightest bit interested. Every morning she made him smoothies and grated veggies for a salad. He never ate them and basically ignored her. She took this very personally and told me that it was ruining her whole raw food experience.

What a waste! Why would you let someone else's behaviour wreck a situation for you?

I suggested that she stop. Stop talking about it. Stop making him food and just stop worrying about it. He still lives on a diet of pies and sausage rolls. He is happy. So is she. (Just for the record — she looks better than he does!)

Trying to force other people to 'do our thing' is such a waste of time. What if instead of spending lots of time trying to get others to do the stuff you want, you just let go? You just let them be? In my experience, one of two things happens:

1.   They continue what they were doing all along — no change.

2.   They suddenly decide on their own terms to do whatever it was that you were trying to get them to do.

Obviously option 2 is better for you, but option 1 is no different than what was already happening, except you have a lot more time and energy because you are no longer worrying about it!

My son started smoking when he was very young. I am talking *very* young — probably around the age of 12. I started to find cigarette burns in his clothes at around the age of 13 or 14.

I was devastated. I hate smoking with a huge passion. Raised by two smokers, I have always been very anti-smoking and I do not understand one single thing about why anyone would do it. Obviously it is an addiction, but why someone would initially voluntarily sign up for something that costs a lot of money, has huge health risks and makes you look and smell terrible is way beyond me.

And yet here I was, with my first-born child a smoker. I did everything. I searched his room. I went through his pockets. No matter how many cigarettes I took away, he just got more.

When he was 16 I gave up. I realised that it was a waste of my time and energy. Ultimately it was his choice, his body and the consequences were his.

It is very empowering to unhook someone from your control. To let it go. I still hate smoking, but I love him. He will work it out. Like everything we go through in parenting, this too shall be a phase. It might be a life-long phase, but I am buggered if I am going to give it any more of my time.

Learning to let go of the things that we cannot control is a life-changer. Another important life-changing behaviour is to teach ourselves to become good receivers.

LEARN TO RECEIVE

Being a good receiver allows us to accept help from others, to allow them to do things for us and to let kindness into our lives.

We all have those friends who will fight ferociously when you offer to pay for coffee or lunch or movie tickets — they find receiving really hard. Some have been raised to believe that 'there is no such thing as a free lunch' and that if you buy them something then at some level they 'owe you'. Some people just cannot handle letting other people do nice things for them.

Yet this is a skill worth learning. Giving and receiving help and kindness is one of the wonderful parts of our human experience. But if you will not allow it to happen, then you miss out.

Start with small things. Learning to receive help and generosity is a great

place to start before you get really brave and actually go out and ask for help.

The next time that someone offers to buy you a coffee or pay for lunch, just be gracious and say 'Thank you, that's very kind.' That is all. Do not go off into a rant about how you owe them for next time or how you will buy them something in exchange. Just say thank you and let the kindness of another wash over you. It is a lovely feeling to let someone do something kind for you.

So many times I see an example of pure kindness and generosity ruined by the other person causing a big scene and fighting the process.

My mum does this. Every time we go anywhere, if I offer to pay for anything she argues and then starts trying to stuff money in my bag or hand. This comes from a life-long ethic of hard work and 'paying your way'. I got angry once and said, 'You gave birth to me, I think that the least I can do is buy you a coffee.' The lady serving us started laughing and said, 'Well, you can't really argue with that!'

Feeling loved and supported is such a nice feeling, and yet often we fight people. We push them away when they try to do nice things, which affirms our belief that we have to do everything ourselves. We need to let people be generous.

LEARN TO ASK FOR HELP

My friend and life coach Marg Culy has taught me so much, and one of the most valuable things I learnt from her was how to accept and ask for help.

Being ferociously independent and determined that I could 'manage anything' was not really working for me. I was stressed and sending out signals to others to back off. No one wanted to approach me because I was running such a good 'super-capable campaign' that everyone ran away.

Asking for help was one of the hardest things I have ever learnt to do. It is easier now, but still gets me feeling a bit icky!

I have learnt that it is *how* you ask that is the secret. Simply saying to someone 'I have a bit of a problem with . . . and wondered if you could help' works well. Phoning someone and starting the phone call with 'Hi, I am a bit stuck and really need your help' is also another great line. It starts the conversation with an expectation of exactly what you want, rather than doing the small-talk dance and then having to find a way to get to your burning need.

The greatest ever line was taught to me by Marg. One day while discussing my huge issue with asking for help, she said, 'By not asking people to help you, you are denying them the opportunity to support you. You are not letting them show their love for you by doing things for you that could make them feel good.'

This is a great way of looking at it! It was a game-changer for me. The irony is that while I was absolutely hopeless at asking for help, I *love* to help other people. If a friend phones and says can you drive me here, pick me up or do this or that for me, I am the first one to help.

I love to help because it makes me feel good. It allows me to show people how much I care about them and how much they mean to me. Yet I was not allowing anyone to do that for me in return.

Two of my closest friends and I were at Marg's house when she was explaining this concept to me. My friends both agreed that they found it hard to ask for help as well — even from each other. While we knew we could count on each other, we had made up stories in our heads that each of us was so super-busy that we couldn't possibly have time to help one another.

Marg suggested that next time I needed some help I was to phone one of my friends and say, 'I have a wonderful opportunity for you', and then follow up with whatever the help was that I needed: 'Would you like to have my children for an hour on Thursday?'

This sounded a lot better than 'I was wondering . . . if you might be able . . . to be around . . . to maybe . . .' stutter stutter stammer stammer.

It was just the line I needed. I phoned my friend the next week and explained the wonderful opportunity that I had for her. She laughed, said that she would be delighted to help and it was done. A week later she phoned me with an 'opportunity'; of course I said yes!

Things just flowed from there. Changing my thinking from 'asking for help' to 'giving someone an opportunity to give' was a game-changer for me.

CHAPTER FOUR

Being wonder-full

Wonderful: inspiring delight, pleasure, or admiration; extremely good; marvellous.

Imagine being able to tell people you were wonderful — full of pleasure, delight and feeling marvellous? To be wonderful you need to be wonder-full — full of wonder. Curious. Excited about life.

I am a glass-overflowing kind of girl. I love to look for positives. Having an expectation of good things happening is a delightful way to live. I love to always believe that something wonderful is going to happen. It makes each day exciting.

Years ago my friend Sally designed me a new business card. After my name were the initials S.F.W. I called her to ask what it meant and she said that it stood for 'So Fucking Wonderful!' I loved that — the best title anyone had ever given to me! Often when people ask me how I am, I reply with 'I am so fucking wonderful.' They nearly fall over! People expect you to say 'I'm OK, or 'Not bad'.

Life has the ability to flatten us out at times. After years of juggling and feeling overwhelmed, some people just lose their spark. Life wears them down. A sign that life has started to grind your good bits away is having rigid patterns of behaviour. People become rigid out of fear. They lose their flexibility. They become stiff and difficult to be with. There is only one way to do anything — their way. The way they have always done it. They are simply too exhausted to be bothered with options. It takes energy to consider options and to look around inside your head for better ways to do things.

After years spent in a state of mental chaos, many women just shut up or shut down. They close their eyes to the possibilities of life. Nothing seems possible — in fact, everything seems impossible.

When you lose your head flexibility, life gets very dull. You go from wonderful to wondering. Wondering what the point is. Wondering why you are doing so much for so little return.

We all get inflexible as we age, but we must keep our heads bendy. Rigid thinking is the beginning of the end.

I am constantly on the lookout for rigid thinking. Keep an eye on your language — you might catch yourself saying 'just because', 'no, that won't work', 'I don't do that' or 'it's not an option'. It can be hard to change, but recognising it is the first step!

BEING ABSORBENT

I think that absorbency is one of the greatest skills a person can have. And the good news is that with a little focus, you can develop it.

Absorbent people are curious. They are both interested and interesting. They want to learn. They want to try new things. They wonder — wonder how things might work, wonder what the options are. Next time you have to make decision, try saying out loud:

- I wonder what would happen if . . .
- I wonder how it would turn out if . . .
- I wonder what my life would look like if . . .

It is my mission to stay absorbent; I like to spend time with absorbent people. If you are not absorbent, then you cannot change the things you don't like about your life. In order to believe in things, you need to be absorbent.

The opposite of an absorbent person is what I call a Formica person. (Formica is a brand of laminate that is used on benchtops and surfaces — stunning if you are wanting a beautiful bench, but not ideal in a person!) Formica people are not absorbent. Anything you pour on them runs straight off. They will waste your time and your energy.

I meet them all the time at my events. They come up and either ask me a question or tell me about a problem they have. The minute you suggest any way forward for them, they will dart back with at least one, and sometimes many, reasons why that will not work.

I have learnt to recognise these people at 20 paces. They are tyre-kickers. There is no point putting effort into them as they cannot absorb your effort. I move on very quickly to another person. There is no point wasting great ideas on Formica people — it's like watering a plastic plant.

I am very generous with my energy. I like to help people, to offer ideas or support. Formica people will not take on anything you suggest — even when they ask for help. There is no benefit in trying to help them! In fact, you will find that Formica people constantly ask for advice, turn up with the same problems over and over and never get anywhere near a solution, even though they are intelligent human beings. No matter how much help or advice you give them, nothing changes.

If you have Formica people around you, it can be very frustrating. Beware of wasting too much time on them. The most effective technique is to ask them 'What are *you* doing about that?' This will hopefully let them see that they have some personal power and that them taking action is what is required.

People become Formica because of fear. Fear has sealed them off. The shut-down Formica person has no faith. They don't believe. They will say 'I can't, 'that won't work', 'that will never happen'.

There is no point wasting great ideas on Formica people — it's like watering a plastic plant.

FORMICA PEOPLE

In my 10 years of dealing with thousands of women, I have realised that there are actually two different groups of Formica people: the FKA and the Shut Down.

FKA (Fucking Know it All)

People who suffer from FKA Disease — 'Fucking Know it All' — will say 'I know', 'I've tried that before', 'I doubt it', 'That doesn't work for me'. They don't trust anything or anyone. They will ask for advice and then bat everything away. Subconsciously they believe they cannot be helped — that they do not deserve a solution. So they keep on proving to themselves that nothing will work.

These people are judgemental and hard to be around. They will argue with you every time you try to suggest any solution. They would rather be right than happy. They will tell you that they are going to be happy — later.

'I'll be happy when . . .' is a disease of the FKA. They like to lecture you on what is happening in their lives but are not interested in your input. Everything you say will be wrong.

They need perspective and fun and something to get excited about. When they are excited by something, their energy will lift and they will be too busy to judge everyone else around them!

I come from a long line of FKAs. You want to see my father, my brother and me all in a room having a battle of 'I know everything' — it is hilarious!

Because of this genetic issue, I have to work hard to keep myself absorbent. To trust the process. Luckily for me, belief and curiosity are also natural traits.

Shut Down

This is a very dangerous state. Shut-down humans are just going through the motions. They are depleted, exhausted. They have stopped believing. They no longer feel like much is possible and are trudging through life, ticking boxes, joylessly. You will be sick of hearing about their problems that they cannot solve.

They have not thought about anything for ages. They are just doing. Not living. Doing the dishes, doing the meals, doing the things on their list. They have given away all of their personal power to just do stuff.

And it's not even stuff that they want to do. They watch TV for hours! They are living mindlessly. They have no idea what interests them or what makes them happy. They just want to get through their list of jobs so that the day can be over.

If you want to help, ask them:

- What are you doing about that?
- What do you want to happen?
- What's your plan?

They need passion, fun and high-vibe people to pull them out of their slump.

Absorbent people
are easier to work
with, are more
fun to be around,
are bendy and
can flow. Formica
people are rigid
and reluctant to
try new things.

GETTING YOUR SHIT TOGETHER

Maybe you are in a slump. You are on the treadmill of feeling awful, so you eat awful things, hang out with awful people and then find you feel really awful. Your behaviour is awful and so is your attitude. Everything that is wrong with your life is someone else's fault. You have well and truly sunk into the shit swamp.

So how are you going to get out? What are you going to do?

Start small. Many of us decide that we want to overhaul our lives and go crazy. We throw out all the food in the fridge, make behaviour charts for the children, clean the house and decide to give up caffeine, sugar and alcohol all in the same week!

For some people this radical approach works. For many it won't. Four hours in, you will decide it is all too hard and revert back to old habits. Having a crazy, unachievable plan will set you up to fail and then you will feel bad again and slip back into the swamp.

I like to pick one thing at a time. Something fairly easy. Start with a lovely bath and a good night's sleep. Then drink eight glasses of water throughout the next day. Then get another good night's sleep. You will feel better bit by bit.

Take a piece of paper and divide it into four squares — Less, More, Stop, Start.

WRITE DOWN:
- What you are going to do less of
- What you are going to do more of
- What you want to stop
- What you want to start.

Often when people decide to change their lives, they are all about getting rid of everything. Lack has never worked for me, and I find that if I *add* things to my life I feel better. Adding *more* time to plan, *more* water to drink or *more* time to exercise might work better.

Rather than going hard and giving things up cold-turkey, you could try writing them in the 'less' column. Having *less* takeaway, *less* alcohol or *less* energy drinks.

Then there is the 'stop' column. This is for the things you are going to stop doing, like stop over-committing yourself or stop gossiping about people. The 'start' column is for things like starting going to the gym or learning a musical instrument.

Start, Stop, Less, More is a great tool for having a mini life-makeover.

YOUR LIFE AS WATER

I was at a retreat once where we were all asked to rate out of 10 how happy we were with our lives. Most people were between 5 and 8, but one woman was a mess. She was incredibly unhappy. Having gone from a controlled career world to the nightmare of having two children very quickly — one with a lot of medical issues — her life was out of control. She had decided that she needed to make some changes but was unsure where to start.

One of the activities we did was to describe our lives as a body of water. One man was a still and calm lake. One woman was a bored, stagnant pond. The stuck woman said she was a river rapid, but she was clinging to the side. She needed to let go and get in the river of her new life.

On the second day we hiked up through some bush and came to a pretty stream with a bridge arching over it. We all selected a stick that we were going to 'let go of'. The idea was to think about something in our lives that we wanted to let go of, to stop, to end, then we took turns at dropping our sticks into the stream.

When I let mine go it took off whizzing downstream until it was out of sight. It was a great exercise — many of us found it useful to physically let go of something that no longer served us.

When the stuck woman approached the bridge she was crying. She did not seem ready to let go of her 'stuff'. She dropped her stick and it went straight into the bank. Stuck! It didn't flow anywhere. It just jammed itself into the side of the bank.

At some level she wasn't ready to move on. She was getting some kind of reward for her stuck behaviour and couldn't seem to get anything to move. She could not allow herself to believe that her life would improve and so her thinking had her stuck. I think that if you can change your thinking, you can change anything.

After a session with one of the coaches at the retreat, we went back to the bridge for her to let go of her stick again. It was only a little stick, but it might as have well been a boulder. The amount of weight — emotional weight — she threw into that stream was enormous. She ditched so much of her thinking, and she went home ready to move forward. It truly was a life-makeover!

When we put our minds to it, we can makeover our lives at any time. Whether we are making big changes by stopping or starting things, or smaller changes by choosing to do less or more things — we are in charge. We can do it.

HOW WOULD YOU DESCRIBE YOUR LIFE AS A BODY OF WATER?

- Is it boring — like a stagnant little pond?
- Is it dramatic — like a wave crashing on a beach?
- Is it beautiful and calm — like a gorgeous lake?
- Is it fast-paced and on the go — like a river rapid?

EMOTIONAL DODGEBALL

One woman I met at the retreat said that she felt like a surfer. Sometimes she caught a good wave, but at other times she would get pounded by another that she had not seen coming. Being pounded is what happens to us when we get hit by emotional balls.

I am not a fan of sports. I never have been. I remember as a child being forced to play team sports on the school field. Each afternoon we would get taken out for a game: long ball, dodgeball, rounders. We would be put into teams and then run, throw and catch. I was one of those girls who closed their eyes when a ball came my way and threw with a limp wrist!

Later in life I came to learn about another type of ball throwing — emotional ball throwing. This is when someone tosses something at you and it hits you emotionally.

Sometimes you see these balls coming and sometimes you don't. On the sports field, the 'mean boys' used to 'brand' me (a hard hit with a tennis ball), usually on the arm or leg. Emotional balls will hit you in the chest or stomach. These big, heavy hits can make you feel sick, sad or numb.

We have all been hit by emotional balls:

- When we realise that we have forgotten something important.
- When we don't do something we said we were going to.
- When someone says something mean or nasty to us.
- When we find out someone has lied to us.

Humans will always have a sense of levelling, when a person tries to put you down so they feel up. Someone who is angry or unhappy may decide that they want you to feel the same.

The school bully is a classic example: the kid who is mean and nasty, going around picking on others, ruining their day just because they are angry inside. Subconsciously they feel better when other people feel bad. Misery loves company!

Over the years I have realised that no one can actually *make* you feel anything. They can try, but you have to buy in. You have to accept the contract. You have to believe them.

That is what emotional dodgeball is all about — avoiding emotional contracts that you don't want!

People who throw emotional balls are often angry, disappointed or jealous. They bundle up their shit and throw it at you. It might be targeted or it might be a random attack. Just like on a basketball court or in the playground, though, you have a choice. You do not have to get hit — you can dodge the ball. And to dodge things successfully you need to see them coming.

Someone who is angry at you because you are not able to attend a lunch with them may throw an emotional ball your way. You can choose to catch the ball and feel terrible that you were not able to be there for your friend. You can carry the ball around, spending all day feeling guilty or sad or both.

Or you can recognise that their disappointment is not yours. It is theirs. None of us like to disappoint a friend, but it happens.

We have busy lives. It is impossible for us to be able to do everything that everyone wants us to do. A line in my favourite poem, 'The Invitation' by Oriah Mountain Dreamer, says: 'Are you prepared to disappoint another to be true to yourself?' Sometimes disappointment cannot be avoided. How we deal with it is the key.

I remember a woman telling me that she would phone her friends and simply say, 'Each day I have to choose someone to let down — someone to piss off. Today is your day. This is not what I had planned but there is nothing I can do!' I'm not sure that this is ideal, but there is definitely some gold in there. Being straight up and telling someone as early as possible 'I am not going to be able to do X. I am really sorry' is the best bet.

Keep it simple. Don't ramble on and on. Just explain that while you fully intended to be able to help/attend/be there, life has come up and it is not now an option.

This is never easy, but it does get easier with practice. It is very empowering to be totally honest with people and to put the important things first. I have heard too many women telling me stories of how they missed their son's soccer game because three weeks earlier they had committed to someone that they would help on a sausage sizzle and did not want to let anyone down.

At your funeral, you will not be remembered for how many sausage sizzles you attended. Your son might well remember the big game that you missed.

When we disappoint someone, understandably they will be hurt. They might be put out. This might sound harsh, but how they deal with their disappointment is not actually your issue. They are an adult and need to learn to cope with life. Don't get contaminated by their emotional energy. Do whatever you can to help — offer to be available at a different time, offer to help in a different way, then let it go. Move on. Carrying around other people's emotional balls is exhausting and painful.

Angry people will throw blame balls. Hate, blame and resentment are all a by-product of our friend anger. If we are angry, we often blame others and resent them.

My daughter caught a hate ball at school one day. On a mufti day a girl told her that her cardigan was ugly. My daughter caught the ball and believed her. She arrived home from school feeling terrible. She was still holding the ball. The problem was not really what the girl had said, but the self-doubt that it brought up. For Ruby to feel bad, she had to at some level believe the girl. She had to wonder if in fact what she was wearing was wrong.

If Ruby was feeling confident and happy, the emotional ball would have missed her. She would have merrily carried on.

Skilled ball-throwers often throw them at people who they know will catch them.

Carrying other people emotionally is very exhausting. We do this with our parents, children (no matter how old) and close friends.

But it is not your responsibility to make other people's lives great. It is theirs. Imagine trying to walk down the street, going about your life, with three rubber balls under your arms. Imagine the struggle. No wonder you feel tired. Not only are you juggling your own roles and responsibilities — it turns out you are also carrying other people's balls.

We have busy lives. It is impossible for us to be able to do everything that everyone wants us to do.

How much of
what weighs you
down is not yours
to carry?

WISHING AND WANTING VERSUS 'I AM'

I meet women every day who are wishing and wanting. They want a new career, they want a new man, they want another child. They wish they had studied more, they wish they had lived their life differently.

Wishing is a waste of time. Something I say to my kids all the time is that hope is not a plan. Don't sit around hoping. Hop up and get going. When people tell me that they hope to change jobs or they hope to go to a foreign country, I get mad. Hope is not a plan.

If there is something that you really want to do, make an 'I am' statement. 'I am' is one of the most powerful ways to start a statement. It sends out a message to the universe that you mean business. That you have set an intention.

The first time I said 'I am' a stylist I thought I was going to throw up — even though I had worked as a stylist for years. I wasn't sure whether I could afford to give myself that title officially.

I now know that this falls under the heading of imposter syndrome. Imposter syndrome is something that many people suffer from. It is very closely linked to Not Good Enough disease and you will find that many people, even highly qualified ones, suffer from it.

Some people do not like to tell people of their plans. They like to squirrel them away alone and then surprise people once they have achieved their goals.

I like to use people to hold me accountable. Find someone you trust. Make an 'I am' statement and then get moving. Do one thing every day that gets you closer to your goal of what you are going to be.

When I first told people I was going to write a book, they looked at me in shock. They said, 'How are you going to do that? What are you going to write about?' I said I didn't know, I just know that *I am* writing a book.

Decide what you want.
Believe you can have it.
Believe you deserve it and
believe it's possible for you.
And then close your eyes every
day for several minutes,
and visualise having what
you already want, feeling the
feelings of already having it.
Come out of that and focus on
what you're grateful for already,
and really enjoy it.
Then go into your day and
release it to the Universe and
trust that the Universe will
figure out how to manifest it.

— Jack Canfield

What other people think of you is none of your business.

— unknown

CHAPTER FIVE

From dramatic to authentic

> If you don't like something,
> change it. If you can't change it,
> change your attitude.

> — Maya Angelou

We have all heard the saying that attitude is everything. So often it is our attitude, not our life, that sucks.

I spoke at a women's conference recently and the opening slide in my presentation said:

Your life will be brilliant if you choose not to be a miserable bitch.

The key word in there is *choose*. So many women *choose* to be miserable. They choose to focus on the drama — on what is going wrong rather than on what is going right.

The problem is that life rewards drama. You get attention. You get help. If you stand around flapping your wings, people will gather.

WHEN LIFE GIVES YOU LEMONS

A few years ago, the *New Zealand Woman's Weekly* ran a story on my children having Type 1 diabetes, to raise awareness about the disease. I received lots of lovely letters and emails from people. One woman came up to me one day and said, 'I had no idea that your life was so hard! You always seem so happy.' I just laughed.

We really have no idea how hard anyone else's life is. People everywhere are dealing with mountains of problems and struggling every day. It is not *what* we deal with but *how* we deal with it that makes us brilliant.

It's important to remember that everyone is dealing with something. That is why it is so important to be kind. If we threw all our problems into the centre of a room and saw everyone else's, we would run in and grab ours back!

I honestly believe that we are never sent anything that we cannot handle. Whatever we are dealt, we can play.

Have you ever noticed that some people have literally nothing to deal with — they have very 'easy' lives — and then others have loads? They have illness and job losses and death all at the same time. And they just have to deal with it.

I think of us as containers. Some of us are big containers that can hold a lot, and some are very small vessels that aren't able to hold much at all. Some people can cope with more than others — and the ones that cope seem to get more shit sent their way.

Unfortunately, you don't get to choose what size container you are. You just get what you get.

And you deal with it — not because you are incredible but because you have to. You have no choice. If your husband walks out, you do not get the opportunity to decide if you want to go through this or not, you just have to get on with it. We all have to deal with the big curve-balls that get thrown our way.

When our third child was diagnosed with Type 1 diabetes, a friend sent me a Facebook message that said: 'God only sends you what you can handle. Apparently he has on file that you are a fucking ninja!' I nearly fell off the hospital bed with laughter.

We all know that life can be a bitch. We all know that there are times when it all seems too much. The problem is that when things are bad we rant and rave and tell everyone and fill the world with our negative sad stories.

Whinging and speaking of our woes is easy. Telling people happy stories or, heaven forbid, sharing our triumphs is not as easily digested by the masses. We have been programmed not to skite, show off or talk about ourselves. I think we need to start talking up the great things we are doing and involved in and ditch our negative drama stories.

Every time you speak of your drama, you give it more energy. Every time another person signs up to listen to your story, your snowball gets bigger. It becomes your focus. Everyone weighs in and it gets larger and larger.

A couple of years ago I slipped two discs in my neck. It was excruciating. I hated having my movement limited and it made life very hard.

For a few weeks I immersed myself in the drama. I wallowed in the self-pity. I told the story to everyone I spoke to. I gave them updates on my pain relief and upcoming medical appointments. It went on and on. It was all anyone asked me about because it was all I was talking about. I was living in a book called *My Neck* by Lisa O'Neill.

And then one day I realised that I was sick of it. I was sick of the questions, sick of hearing myself talk about it. I wanted it to be over. So I decided it was. From that moment on I changed my mind. When people asked about my neck, I said 'It's much better thanks' or 'It's great.' This was in fact a lie — it still hurt like hell — but I was not interested in it being the biggest thing in my life anymore.

Every time someone brought it up I changed the subject. I moved on. My neck was no longer the focus.

Now this is not a story of spontaneous healing. I still continued taking the painkillers and anti-inflammatories, I continued seeing my osteopath and massage therapist. *But I dropped the drama.*

It changed the way I felt. I felt better.

This was an important lesson for me. We are all in charge of how we feel. We can actually decide how we feel about things.

Sometimes the
only thing we
can change is
our mind.

LOOK FOR THE GOOD BITS

For so many of us, our lives are not what we thought they would be — we never guessed that we could be in the situation that we are in. Partners leave, people die, our bodies get sick. Letting go of what you think your life is 'supposed' to be and learning to celebrate what it is is the secret.

In 2000, my cousin was killed in an avalanche in Japan. It was awful. My aunty and uncle lost their precious son. They lost a future daughter-in-law, they lost grandchildren. My other cousin lost his brother and best friend. That mountain took a lot away from them.

For the past 16 years I have watched my aunty deal with this tragedy. She has ridden the waves of grief.

She has no idea how wise she is. We were talking on the phone recently about someone she knew who was having a rough time, and she said, 'Life is not all peaches and cream. Sometimes you just have a bowl of peaches with no bloody cream. But you just have to be grateful for your peaches.'

My daughter was in the car while we were speaking and she said, 'Wow! I love how positive Aunty Gaynor is, Mum. She has been through the hardest stuff of anyone I know and she still says lovely things like that.'

My aunty is one of those people who, despite life dealing her so many shitty cards, can still see the good bits.

In my first book, *Look Gorgeous Be Happy*, I wrote about the glad game, created by author Eleanor H. Porter in the book *Pollyanna*. I like to play the glad game. It's really simple: you just find things to be glad about. Being glad about stuff makes you happy. The gladness will show in your face.

Talking about your gladness is much nicer than talking about your dramas. Try each day to focus on a good story — something good that has happened in the news (if you can find it!), something nice that someone has done, something kind or helpful. Spreading stories of kindness and people helping people makes you nicer to be around.

Unfortunately it is not easy. Repeating bad stories is easy — jumping on the drama train and adding your five cents' worth to the world's latest disaster is a piece of cake! Make an effort to share good stories, to do good things and to be around good people. The dark side is tempting, but it won't make your life better!

10 per cent
of life is what
happens to you.
90 per cent is
how you react
to it.

HANDLING STRESS

Stress is something we all have to deal with. Every day there are any number of things than can and will cause you stress.

I have trained myself to deal with stress. To not let myself react.

When you react to people, you give away your personal power. And personal power is exactly what you need at times of stress. Hold on to as much of it as you can.

When we become physically stressed, our cortisol levels rise, our heart rate increases and our blood pressure gets out of whack. Instructing your head how you want to deal with a situation will stop your body from starting a physical reaction.

I have three tricks for dealing with stress:

1. First, I tell myself, repeatedly, that everything happens for a reason and that at some level this must be for my greater good. I honestly believe this — the hard bit is that the reason is not always obvious to us. When things don't go to plan we have the opportunity to learn about ourselves, to change our direction and to grow stronger.

2. Second, I physically remove myself from the situation and do some slow, deep breathing. Slowing down your breathing will calm your body and reduce the impact of stress on your body. If you feel calm, you will be calm. If you can control your breathing, you can control your life.

3. The third part of my stress response is to acknowledge how I feel. I love to swear out loud about how I am feeling. Speaking your truth and shouting about how you feel is very good for both your physical and your mental health. Internal stress will eventually express itself in your physical body. Writing a letter (that you never send), yelling alone or actually confronting the person who has caused you the stress are all great ways to acknowledge how you feel.

Try to be really clear about how you are feeling. Are you angry or actually deeply sad? Do you feel silly or humiliated? The clearer you can become about where you stand, the faster you can deal with the issue.

DRAMA QUEENS

Drama loves attention. Drama never just walks into your life — you create it, invite it or join it.

People who constantly seek drama will find it! They can turn anything into a drama and then they want to give you constant updates.

As I mentioned earlier, be very careful not to be a subscriber to their issues. These people are exhausting to be around and, quite frankly, you need to chop them off at the knees. Do not show any interest. Change the subject. Tell them something positive — they will hate that! They want to wallow in the 'unsolvable problem'.

The problem for the poor old drama queen is that she has no other way to get any attention than to create dramas. These people run around being 'busy' and talking endlessly about whatever their latest drama is. They need to shut up and get interesting.

THE ALTERNATIVE: BEING INTERESTING

Being interesting is one of the greatest things we can ever be. Being interesting means that you can hold someone's attention.

I loathe boring people. I have a very short attention span and can smell a boring person at 50 paces. Dramatic people used to hold my attention, but these days I have a low tolerance. They are self-absorbed *and* boring — what a combination!

SO, I WANT YOU TO THINK ABOUT HOW INTERESTING YOU ARE:

- What have you done recently that is interesting?
- What do you find interesting?
- Who do you think is interesting?

Books, places and people can all lead us to interesting topics. What may interest you might be of no interest to the person next to you — but that is precisely how this stuff works. You find something you are interested in and

then you find other people who are interested in the same thing and then your life gets interesting!

I have a gorgeous friend called Sally who is a hilarious and completely unique combination of hardcore and beautifully girly. She has always been keen on guns and shooting but is also one of the most creative people that I know, who can turn a piece of fabric into literally anything you can imagine.

A few years ago, after a little bit of research, she found a group called Cowboy Action Shooters. These people dress in period costume and have shooting competitions with real pistols. This is the ultimate combination of everything that Sally loves! She sews incredible costumes and gets to hang out with people who love the same things as her. None of her usual friends are interested in these hobbies, but now she has a completely new set of friends who share her passion and interest.

Years ago I was visiting a friend in her seventies who told me she had decided to join a singing group. They also performed small plays and entertained people. I asked her if she had always loved to sing and act and she said no, not at all! I was curious, so I asked her why she had joined the group. She said, 'Well, I was worried that I wasn't very interesting so I thought I should do something about it.' I love this: at 74 years old she had suddenly decided that she needed to make herself more interesting!

I met another amazing women in a Farmers store one day. She was carrying a load of clothing and I asked her if I could be of some help. She said she was buying travel clothes for a trip she was going on. I asked her where she was going and she said, 'I have decided to take myself away.' She said she wasn't happy and so had decided to do something about it.

How cool is that! I spent the rest of the day thinking about where I would take myself.

I am sure that some of you reading this are thinking 'God, if only I had the time to go and make myself interesting . . . I can barely fit in everything now!'

Making time to make yourself interesting is vital to your vitality. It will make you happier, more alive and give you stuff to look forward to.

People often think that happy or interesting people are lucky, that being that way just happens for them. Not true. To be good at anything, you have to work at it. Being happy takes work. It takes focus on what actually makes you happy.

Being interesting is the same. To be interesting, you need to know what interests you.

YOUR PHD (PERSONAL HAPPINESS DEVELOPMENT)

So many busy people get so busy in the doing that they lose track of what actually interests them. They know what they do each day but not what sets them alight.

When I mentor clients I suggest that they create their own PHD (Personal Happiness Development), from the School of You. For example, the School of Lisa's curriculum covers poetry, film, alternative therapies, dance, medicinal food, comedy and lots of other things that interest me.

If you had a week alone, where you had to do something each day from 9 a.m. to 5 p.m., anything at all — what would you do? What would your PHD be in? What would you do just because you loved it?

When we do things that we find interesting, we improve our emotional energy. We feel better.

Doing something we really want to is such a nice change from just doing what we have to all day. The responsibilities of being an adult mean that many of us are constantly weighed down with shoulds and have-tos instead of wants. Doing what we want makes us feel powerful and free and alive. But first you have to work out what it is you want to do!

Make a list. Write down all the things that interest you and things that you would like to do. Do not judge your list. Do not waste time thinking about what your friends, family and children are going to say about your list. Just make a list of things that *you* want to do.

Some of these things will be small. Some will be big. Some will cost a lot of money. Some you can do at home. But as the slogan goes, just do it. Actually just do *anything* — interesting is always a better option than just busy.

BEING A MARTYR

Constantly giving in to other people to gain social approval is not a smart way to live your life — and yet so many women do it. They spend their days running around as if they were playing a virtual game, gathering points for all the 'things that they do for others'. When we do more for others than we do for ourselves, we create an imbalance.

Doing good things, being kind and being generous are wonderful traits that should be encouraged, but it all comes back to the intent. Why are you doing such wonderful things?

Are you doing things to genuinely help the people around you, or are you doing them for recognition and glory? How many of these good deeds would you do if they were all anonymous and no one ever found out you'd done them?

Doing something kind for someone else is lovely, but if it is not done for the right reasons it can breed resentment. There is a price to pay when we indulge in martyr behaviour — to the outside world we look great, but on the inside we are simmering with resentment. We feel angry and undervalued. Ain't no one got time for that!

Sometimes in an effort to get some recognition and attention we exhaust ourselves for no gain. The imbalance comes when we give more than we receive.

Resentment is such an ugly disease — it is like acid that burns and stings your insides. One of the biggest builders of resentment is not speaking your truth.

SPEAKING YOUR TRUTH

Speaking your truth and actually saying out loud how you feel is very empowering — and, I might warn you, mildly addictive!

We need to be honest with the people in our lives about how we feel. Yet so often we don't. We sit on our thoughts and feelings because we do not want to hurt others. Instead we hurt ourselves. We hold on to so much.

I have always been very verbal. Honestly speaking, I like the sound of my own voice! I have opinions that I think are great!

In order to protect other people's feelings, we so often hold our opinions back. We swallow them so we don't offend anyone else.

The people in our lives do not deserve to be in our lives if they cannot hear our truths. I was fortunate to hear Neale Donald Walsch (author of *Conversations With God*) speak about 15 years ago in Wellington. He was talking about being authentic in our relationships when a woman stood up to ask how being authentic was going to help her relationship. Walsch replied that without knowing more details about her actual relationship he was not really able to answer that, and offered to speak with her privately after the event. She then blurted out, in front of a thousand people, that she no longer thought she loved her husband and had no idea what to do about it. Walsch very calmly suggested that she should go home and tell her husband how she was feeling. The woman said that she couldn't do that because she didn't think that he would cope. Walsch said that wasn't her problem. He did not deserve a place in her life if he could not handle her truth.

Wow! I was blown away! How good is that? It takes me straight to the scene in the 1992 movie *A Few Good Men* with Jack Nicholson when he shouts — 'You can't handle the truth!'

So here is a thought — can the people in your life handle your truth?

First you have to work out what your truth is . . . or maybe you already know?

I have a very wise friend who has a gay son. This boy was wearing dresses at five years old, so it was no surprise to anyone when he came out. But before that happened, I was intrigued by why my friend had never had a conversation with her son about him being gay. I said 'Don't you want to ask him about it?', and she replied, 'No. It is his truth and he will get to it when he is ready. You have to be ready. Once he says it out loud there is no turning back. He will know when he is ready.' Bloody wise woman! I love that. Instead of forcing or coercing or prodding, she just let him be. She let him get to his truth when he was ready. She knew that it was *his* truth, not hers.

So maybe you have your truth but its time has not yet come. Maybe it needs to percolate a little bit more before you hit the world with it. Just keep asking yourself how you feel, and listen to the rosiness that you get from within.

START TO ASK YOURSELF:

- How do I feel about that?
- What do I know about that?
- What do I think about that?
- What have I decided about that?
- What is my opinion on what is happening?

Being brave enough to voice our own opinions is a big deal. When you say what you honestly think, you put yourself on the edge of your safety zone. People may choose to disagree; people may choose to ridicule you or judge you on your beliefs.

Stating your truth is something that will change your life. In the Bible it says 'then you will know the truth, and the truth will set you free.' American feminist and journalist Gloria Steinem is quoted as saying 'The truth will set you free but first it will piss you off'! So true.

You see, the truth can be hard — being honest with ourselves is the hardest bit to get our heads around. Then we need to get brave and share our truth.

If speaking your truth is a new thing for you, I would like to make a few suggestions. Get really clear about what your truth is before sharing it. Whipping a cake out of the oven before it is cooked is not a good idea. Let the cake cook. Let it cool. Then serve it. Once we have put something 'out there', it cannot be taken back.

American psychotherapist Dr Brand Blanton wrote two great books on this topic. *Radical Honesty* and *Practising Radical Honesty* are great reads for anyone wanting to let themselves be free by telling their truth.

WHEN TO KEEP YOUR OPINIONS TO YOURSELF

In my years working as a stylist, I was constantly asked for my opinion on what people were wearing, how they looked and what they could fix. That is fine when you are being paid for your opinion, but outside of work I had a rule: I only offered my advice if it was asked for. I never rock up to a woman on the street and say 'Your top is bloody awful', but if she asks me 'What do you think of my top?' I tell her straight!

It is important to me to be honest and authentic, but I do not see it as my right to run around the country handing out my opinions. 'Opinions when asked' is my motto. I have even been asked for my opinion and then asked the person if they really want it — if they ask, they will get. I will tell them exactly what I think because they have asked me. They have officially invited me to say what I think!

We all have people in our lives who are full of opinions. They have non-stop ideas on how we can live our lives.

It comes as a shock to these people that we do not want their opinions. And just as empowering as it is to speak your truth, it is also very empowering to not

listen to other people's version of your truth: people who will tell you what you should be doing, what you should be wearing, how you should be running your life. Tell them that you are not interested. Thanks, but no thanks.

The phrase 'I think . . .' is a great place to start if you are invited to give your opinion. 'I think that you would look better in a longer skirt' is quite different from 'You shouldn't wear short skirts'. The 'I think' adds your ownership. It is what *you* think and they have invited your opinion in.

I get really cross with people who bombard you with advice that you have not asked for. I think that this is arrogant and rude. So many times I have been helping a woman in a dressing room and another woman also trying on clothes will start telling us what she thinks of what is being worn.

Once I was working with a woman who was very precious. She had a lot of issues around her body confidence and self-esteem, and I was trying to get her to see that her body was nowhere near as bad as she thought. She arrived wearing enormous tents that made her look bigger than she was.

I spent over an hour gently coaxing this woman into trying some new colours and styles and she was starting to come out of her shell. She went outside the dressing room to look in the large mirror when a woman in the changing room next door stuck her head around and said, 'I don't think that's very flattering — I don't like it at all.' This woman, a complete and total stranger, had just undone all my good work! My customer was reduced to tears and my time was wasted, all because of some know-it-all with a big gob.

AUTHENTICITY

Authenticity is really, really important to me. Before we can be authentic we need to know who we are, what we believe. Authentic people are original. They are themselves, rather than being a cardboard cut-out copy of someone else.

To be truly original, we have to let go of all the stuff that we think is us. As we grow and learn, we gather and collect information. We collect opinions, beliefs and thoughts, and our heads become a filing cabinet full of other people's stuff.

Clearing out this stuff is part of us growing into ourselves. We start to form our own opinions and beliefs and start to really know who we are.

Authenticity can take years. It can take a long time to sift through your filing cabinet — delving into the 'greatest hits' of all the beliefs you have been given.

Listen to what you say. Think about things as they pop up. Detaching yourself from the thoughts of others is empowering.

Each little piece of paper in your mental filing cabinet can be read, examined and then dealt with. Maybe it's a load of bollocks; maybe it's something you resonate with. Consider your thoughts on each one before you decide what to do with it.

After listening to what you say to yourself and then thinking about what you hear and see, you will start to get to your truth. Then comes the speaking. Speaking your truth.

Authenticity is
the daily practice
of letting go of
who we think
we're supposed to
be and embracing
who we are.

— Brené Brown

CHAPTER SIX

Big Elephants

After a little baby elephant is born, it spends 12 years with its herd. It is taught everything that it needs to know about life, how to keep itself safe and how to survive in the big wide world. Between the ages of 12 and 14 years old, the young elegant will set off to make its own herd — to be its own person (elephant!). The success of this elephant depends on how well it was taught by its big elephants.

This is pretty much the same for us humans. How well prepared we are and how well we function in society depends on how good our Big Elephants are. When we are young our Big Elephants are usually our parents, aunties, uncles and grandparents, and as we grow up teachers, role models and other mentors take over.

When I see people in the media and on the streets, I wonder how good their Big Elephants were. What were they taught? How well were they taught it?

Whatever we grow up with, we think is normal. If your parents sat around playing cards or made cakes for your neighbours, then that is what you believe is normal and acceptable. If you grew up with your parents selling drugs to the neighbourhood, then you think that is normal. We believe our Big Elephants.

When I ask people what they learnt from their parents, they often tell me things like cooking, sewing or building — actual tasks and skills. I am really wanting to know what they *really* learnt – did they learn to be independent because their parents were so unreliable? Did they learn to be useless because their parents were so overbearing?

What if you don't like or get on with your Big Elephants? If you have trouble relating to your family members,

ASK YOURSELF:

- What have I got to learn here?
- What is this person teaching me about myself?
- Or are they showing me what I do not want to do or be?

Your Big Elephants might be extended family, mentors or coaches. Anyone who teaches or guides you.

ASK YOURSELF:

- When I was growing up, who were my Big Elephants?
- How good were they?

- What did they teach me?
- Who are my Big Elephants now?

As we get older we outgrow our Big Elephants, and I feel that it is really important to find new ones. I am always on the lookout for people I can learn from, who can teach me, push me and guide me.

If you are feeling stuck or suffering from 'Big Elephant Disappointment', then get out there and find someone new. Life coaches, business mentors and teachers are all worth engaging to work out what is next for you. To be a life-long learner, you need teachers.

ASK YOURSELF:
- What would I like to learn?
- What would I like to be good at?
- Who is good at these things?
- Who could help or teach me?

We have so much to learn and some incredible people around us to learn it from, if we take the time to look. One of the saddest parts of modern living is that we are not as connected to people as we could be. We text instead of phoning. We email instead of meeting people. We miss out on so much when we limit our human interactions, including the chance to learn and grow.

CHOOSING YOUR PARENTS

I honestly believe that children choose their parents — that before we are conceived we select our Big Elephants for whatever we need to learn in this life. Maybe your soul decides that it needs to learn to be self-sufficient. You may then choose a set of hopeless parents, just so you have to learn to fend for yourself and become self-sufficient more quickly than if you chose caring, thoughtful parents who did everything for you.

Some people seem to have made interesting parent choices — they seem to have chosen people who have nothing to offer. I believe that everyone who comes into your life has something to offer and something to teach you — the secret is in being able to recognise it.

FINDING A BIG ELEPHANT

In every area of my life I have always tried to find a Big Elephant to lead me. Having older, wiser friends who were a few years ahead of me on the parenting journey was very valuable, for example.

You need someone who can reassure you that things will be OK, that your current crisis is not the end. Often when we are dealing with things on our own we can lose sight of the size of the problem. I love the saying that a problem shared is a problem halved.

But remember, getting someone else's perspective on your problems is good — but only as good as the person you share it with! Well-meaning bad advice will not help. It will take up valuable time. This is where a good-quality Big Elephant will be of enormous help.

What would you like to learn? What are you hopeless at? Whether you want help to get your baby to sleep or advice on how to manage your LinkedIn profile, you can find someone out there to teach you.

Sometimes you need to pay Big Elephants. They do not always just come free with your life! Paying experts to help you can save you a lot of time and eventually money. They can also help make your juggle smoother.

For example, I have a computer man who can update and transfer files in one-tenth of the time it takes me to stuff it up and start all over again. I also have a mentor whom I speak to monthly who challenges me and holds me accountable for the things that I am working on in my business. I have achieved so much more with him leading me than if I was doing it on my own.

So many women want to change their lives but need clarity on what it is that they want. Find a career coach or a mentor or a life coach who will push you and guide you through your changes. If your marriage is hard, go and speak to a counsellor. If your kid is out of control, go and get some advice. If you want to get fit but hate exercise, pay a personal trainer to keep you on track. Do not buy into the argument that you should be able to do it on your own. Don't be an island. Be smart. Get help in the areas of your life that need it.

MR WALKER

One of my most beautiful Big Elephants was a man called Mr Walker. Sometimes the universe sends you people as gifts and he was just that — a delightful, intelligent and creative gentleman whom I had the privilege to meet through mutual friends.

When I met Mr Walker I was 26 and he was 67. He was a film-maker and photographer and we seemed to have a never-ending list of things to talk about. I loved to ask him questions and listen to his theories on a wide range of topics. He had a lovely, formal uptightness to him and the most brilliant sense of humour, that you never really saw coming. I always called him Mr Walker and he always called me Miss Brown (my maiden name) — even after I was married!

Every Wednesday I would visit him and we would have Earl Grey tea and shortbread. On Fridays at lunchtime I took him fried rice and ginger beer. Our conversations covered topics from art to people to philosophy to lighting. I have always been a very creative person but had not chosen a very creative family, so sitting and discussing light and form and design with this clever man made me so happy.

Mr Walker had grown up in Levin — he had lived in the same house his whole life. He grew up in the house as an only child, lived with his parents until they died and then stayed in the house.

He was born in the 1930s and by the age of 12 knew that he was gay. But it did not define him, and while he was quiet about his sexuality he certainly never hid it. He simply didn't see it as a defining part of his life.

One of my favourite things Mr Walker taught me came from a flippant comment I made about someone being 'gay'. He pulled me up straight away and asked me what that meant. I said it didn't mean anything, I was just saying that this man was openly gay and therefore was obviously attracted to men. Mr Walker looked over his cup of Earl Grey tea and me and said 'It's a bit like finding out if someone eats broccoli, isn't it?'

'What?!' I said, completely confused about where this conversation was going.

Mr Walker replied: 'Who someone prefers to have a sexual relationship with is about as interesting as whether or not they like to eat broccoli. What *is* important about people is are they creative, are they intelligent and are they kind.'

I thought that was very true — though I often couldn't help myself and on our outings would point out other possible 'broccoli eaters', and he would tell me off!

I have never been fazed by who or what people are, but Mr Walker taught me a very valuable lesson about not putting people in boxes or compartments. He died 12 years ago and I still miss him.

Mr Walker taught me a very valuable lesson about not putting people in boxes.

BECOMING A BIG ELEPHANT

I remember waking up on my husband's thirtieth birthday and thinking 'Shit, we are getting old — we need to have a baby!'

We had always known we would have children, but life had become busy. We were both travelling a lot for work and the years were creeping by.

Within three weeks I had a blue line on that stick. I was pregnant. Holy shit!

I loved being pregnant. I wandered around like a mobile miracle, happy to let people in the supermarket touch my glorious belly. I studied and read and joined antenatal groups to find out as much as I could. I was obsessed with my new role as a parent.

I hadn't really been around too many babies and had decided that this kid would just slot into our fabulous lives and we would carry right along.

I was not prepared for the emotions that came with the baby. It was like being in love times one million. I was besotted. I was also a little deranged, and honestly thought that I was the only person who had ever created such a miracle. Mark and I sat on the couch for weeks just staring at him!

I was incredibly lucky to have some stunning Big Elephants in this part of my life. Jane Stojanovic and Liz Jull were my midwives. They were wise, calm women who taught me to trust my body and to trust the process. I had four magical birth experiences, which I put down to their fine coaching and me feeling so incredibly safe and well supported.

I found birth to be a very powerful and empowering experience. I had grown and birthed a human — I now had no doubt that there was nothing I couldn't do! I truly felt like I was capable of anything.

BIRTHING EXPERIENCES

I have spent years listening to birth stories, and feel that for many women their birthing experience has the ability to change their lives. Having a powerfully positive birth experience can have an incredible impact on your life, just as having a traumatic one can.

None of us can control the experience that we have once another human decides to come out of our bodies, but I spend a lot of time urging women to surround themselves with powerful, confident, positive people while they are pregnant. Having people around you who are negative and full of fear will do nothing for your state of mind. My birthing theories were:

- I was designed to do this.
- More goes right than goes wrong.

Relaxing and trusting my body to do its job with the support of professionals was a far better way than being riddled with fear and clenched so tight that nothing had a chance of exiting!

Three of my babies were born at home, and I met some wonderful women through the home-birth world. They were calm and kind and seemed to have their priorities in order. They home-schooled and grew their own food and made their own clothes. I would arrive in high heels with my designer nappy bag on my way to a meeting and they never judged me. They taught me the 'good for you' philosophy — they would never pass judgement about anything anyone did, they would just say 'Good for you'. I love that. If you wanted to breastfeed your kids until they were five years old — good for you. If you wanted to vaccinate your children — good for you. Whatever was 'good for you', they supported.

About four weeks after Oscar arrived, my midwife Jane popped in. I was busy. I was tidying and trying my hardest to get everything (me, the house and the baby) to look perfect. Jane growled. She sent me to bed. It was 9 a.m.! She told me that my house didn't matter: the only job I had to do was make milk for my son. She tucked Oscar and me into bed and left with instructions that I was not to move. At 4 p.m. she came back to check on me!

It was the greatest gift. I was trying really hard to be on top of everything but I had all my priorities up the spout. This was something Jane had seen often. Exhausted women don't make milk. My job was to love and feed this baby — everything else could wait.

I took Jane's advice very seriously . . . I have never done housework since! She asked me where I kept my vacuum cleaner and I thought she was going to vacuum for me — but instead she dumped it in the middle of the lounge and said 'Leave it there and people will think that you were just about to vacuum. They will probably offer to do it for you.' That vacuum cleaner lived in the middle of the lounge for five years!

Another wonderful influence at this time was my friendly Plunket nurse, Keren Lusty. I was so excited about her visits. I would tidy the house and bake and try really hard to look like Mother of the Year. I would have Oscar dressed in all his best clothes and sit and wait for her arrival. Exhausting! (At this point I was still suffering quite badly from 'What will people think' disease!)

The first time Keren came for my home visit I was really nervous. I had in my head that Plunket was like the baby police. I wanted a gold star. I would have liked a certificate. When Keren left she asked if I had any questions and I told her I was worried that I wouldn't know what to do with Oscar — that I didn't really know that much about babies and now I had one living in my house!

I was a self-confessed control freak and found that the hardest thing about having this new baby to care for was not being in control. Of anything. I could not control when he slept, I could not control anything about him. I was so unsure about everything.

Keren turned around and said, 'Lisa, you will always know what to do because you are the mother. Just follow your instincts.' That statement changed my life. I walked around the house feeling like the President of the United States who had just arrived at the White House!

I knew what to do. I was the mother. From that moment on I learnt to stop trying to control things and to work with my instincts.

Life doesn't come with a manual, it comes with a mother.

So now that you have become a Big Elephant yourself, who is your go-to person for parenting advice? Your mum will be invaluable when you are trying to wind a young baby, but may be of no use around internet boundaries when your kids are older! One of the saddest things about our modern times is the lack of community and sharing that we now do. With so many mothers working, we miss out on the sharing and wisdom that was traditionally handed down from older women to younger women. I believe that women need to share more wisdom, to give more support to each other as we navigate the millions of phases that parenthood throws at us.

A few years ago I was on holiday in Samoa. We drove past a huge gathering of around 60 women all sitting in a huge waterfall, chatting and breastfeeding. There were little children everywhere and women sitting sharing their knowledge. It reminded me of a playgroup that I attended when my children were little. There were lots of mothers, lots of children and lots of wonderful older women who were always available to hold a baby, offer some advice or make a cup of tea.

I have some wonderful friends who have been amazing leaning posts for me as a mother. Some are a few years older than me. Speaking to a mother who has already dealt with the things that you are dealing with allows some wonderful insights and wisdom to be shared.

BEING A MOTHER BEAR

I remember the first time I experienced my 'Mother Bear'. Oscar, my eldest son, was about nine hours old. I went to sleep in my hospital bed and woke up after two hours to find my baby was gone. I dashed down to the nursery in a state of panic. I got there to find a lovely old midwife feeding Oscar formula from a bottle. With the best of intentions, she had taken him out of my room so I could sleep.

She asked me who my midwife was. I told her Jane. The minute she heard Jane's name she said, 'Oh dear, she won't be happy.' I wasn't sure what to think. I knew that I was perfectly aligned with all of Jane's views on babies, birth and feeding, so if Jane wasn't happy, I wasn't happy.

But I wasn't just unhappy, I was wild. This woman had no right to take my precious, brand-new baby and fill him up with some fake milk without my permission. I had this overwhelming feeling of anger and rage and of total protection for this little human that I had grown.

I grabbed Oscar and headed back to my room.

It's the same feeling I get now when someone has wronged my child, when someone is mean or unfair. There is nothing more powerful than an angry mother. The instinct to protect is so primal and so strong that it needs to be obeyed. Except so many parents don't. They calm down and then tell their children to deal with it instead of fighting and taking these people on.

The reason so many parents do this is that they are more concerned with what other people will think than with protecting the spirit of their children. Now, I am not talking about constantly fighting your children's battles or never letting them deal with life's consequences, but a child needs to know that someone will fight for them and no one knows your child better than you.

I have had many experiences in the past 17 years where I have stood up to teachers, coaches and other parents. Teaching your children that they should put up with bad behaviour is not going to teach them to be powerful adults. Stand up for them. Teach them to stand up for themselves.

A lot of parents
will do anything
for their kids —
except let them
be themselves.

— Banksy

CHAPTER SEVEN

Energy is everything

Not looking after yourself is dumb. Trashing your energy and ability to be dynamic and vital is about as clever as a farmer poisoning his own crops. You are your best asset. When your energy levels are good, you have a much better chance of supporting, carrying and providing for those around you.

I am my company's best asset. (Actually, I am my company's only asset!) I cannot afford to not be in peak condition. Now, I am not talking peak athletic condition. I am talking *in the best condition that I can be in for me*. Fit for purpose. Fit for being me.

WHEN ARE YOU AT YOUR BEST?

For me to be fit for purpose, I need to be well rested, have the right fuel and be feeling happy and relaxed. Making sure that my needs are met is vital for me to do everything that I do for so many others.

Before you can create the perfect platform for you to thrive, you need to know what it is that you need. What are the things that you need to be at your best?

For me personally, I need:

1. **To look good.** Looking my best raises the vibration of my energy and makes me feel more alive. When I look good I feel good. Simple.

2. **Cash.** When I do not have access to money I don't feel prosperous. Cash makes me feel powerful and safe.

3. **Sleep.** I need a lot of sleep. Resting my body is a luxury I cannot afford to not have. Rest is best.

What are the things that make you feel more like you?

ASK YOURSELF:
- What are the three things that I need to be at my best?

YOUR HOT-AIR BALLOON

Imagine yourself as a huge hot-air balloon. You have a basket full of responsibilities. All your roles are in the basket. You are a daughter, a mother, a sister, a lover, a friend, a colleague, an employee, an aunty. The fuel that is going to determine your energy — and how high you can fly — is the quality of your sleep, diet and health.

So what fills you up? What will add air to your balloon? Make a list.

The things that fill me up are: weekend retreats, watching movies, reading inspiring books, playing with my cat, shopping, massage, laughing with friends, being with my children, staying in luxury accommodation.

I need to do one of these things every day. It keeps my balloon up. It makes me feel like I matter.

The fuel that is going to determine how high you can fly is the quality of your sleep, diet and health.

Do whatever you need to get more sleep. Your life will improve.

THE IMPORTANCE OF SLEEP

The quality and quantity of your sleep has an enormous impact on your energy. The right amount of sleep is critical to your performance as a human being.

There has been so much research and writing on the benefits of sleep in recent years. I have always been a hefty sleeper. I love a good sleep. I am often the first into bed in our house. Sleeping is the most restorative thing that we can do for ourselves. So why do we actively seem to avoid it?

You will not become a super-hero by not sleeping. There are no tired super-heroes! And yet people wear their tiredness as a badge of honour. 'Barely slept last night', 'Only got two hours' sleep'.

I do not find these statements impressive. Being tired is dumb. It is not something to be proud of.

I also find it unprofessional and arrogant to arrive at work tired. We all have nights when things do not go well and we have a bad sleep, but people who constantly turn up complaining about their lack of sleep make me cross. Exhaustion is not cool. Turning up to work well rested and ready to give your best for the next eight hours is cool. Sort your shit out. Go to bed.

There are times in your life when you will be tired. That bone-tired feeling of having a newborn baby. The broken sleep, the hours awake in the night. I can remember standing in the supermarket one day feeling like the floor was moving up towards me, I was so exhausted. I would stare at people while they talked to me, having no idea what they were saying!

Now we all know that having young children is exhausting and so the smart thing to do when you are in this phase is to plan some sleep time. Make it a priority.

If you have a young family, sleep when your children sleep. Nap with them in the afternoon. I used to love going to bed with my toddlers in the afternoons. The other option was to dash around the house, vacuuming and tidying. No thanks! The house will wait. Clean up when they move out.

The early years are about survival. And sleep is essential to your survival.

An adult between the ages of 19 and 55 needs eight hours' sleep every night. If you miss one hour each night, by the end of the week you have literally lost one whole night's sleep!

You will die from sleep deprivation before food deprivation. It takes two weeks to starve, but 10 days without sleep can kill you!

When you sleep, your brain recharges. Your cells repair themselves. Your body releases important hormones.

American author and businesswoman Ariana Huffington, who wrote the books *Thrive* and *The Sleep Solution*, speaks about 'sleeping your way to the top'. Sleep is not a luxury. It is essential.

Here are some tips for getting more, better-quality sleep:

- Plan for sleep. Set an alarm for when you need to go to bed rather than when you need to get up.
- Allow 30 minutes before bed to wind down. No phone or iPad. Shower, read, relax.

YOU ARE WHAT YOU EAT...

What you eat has a huge impact on how you feel. Weighing down your body with heavy carbohydrates, sugars and foods that put pressure on your immune system will not help you to be the best person you can be.

Now, I am not saying we should all be living on a diet of kale and mung beans, but eating regularly and having some idea about what works for your body and what doesn't is a really good start.

I like to eat foods that my body finds easy to process. It just seems to make sense. If you love and care about yourself, why would you give your body hard work to do? If you play nice to your body, it will play nice back!

Twelve years ago I was diagnosed with coeliac disease. My immune system sees gluten as a big threat. I have spent a lot of time researching the effects of gluten on our bodies, and whether you are coeliac or not I believe many people could do with less of it in their diets.

Our modern-day diets of heavily processed foods mean that many people are having more than eight servings of gluten each day — it's hidden everywhere, in ham, sauces, salad dressings, muesli bars, etc.

My body is also not very accepting of dairy products. The more I remove from my diet, the happier my body seems to be. For the past six months I have been eating organic meat, veggies, eggs, nuts and berries. That's it. Very simple. My energy levels have increased. I sleep better, I feel better.

Rumbling tummies, long-winded fart sessions and no energy are all signs that your body may not be reacting well to things you have eaten. I have found that meals high in protein sustain me for longer and have got me off the carb – sugar see-saw.

With three Type-1-diabetic children and five coeliacs in the house, I have been forced to be more aware of what we eat. Having never dieted or calorie counted, I was blown away at what I learnt when we had to learn to 'carb count' to manage my children's diabetes.

Carb counting is calculating the exact amount of carbohydrates in everything that you eat.

For those of us with functioning pancreas glands, our clever bodies somehow manage to read the exact number of carbs that have been digested and provide the perfect matching amount of insulin to allow the food to be broken down. However, because Type 1 diabetics have no ability to make

insulin, the process requires lots of time, knowledge and a calculator! All food must be precisely weighed and measured to ensure that the correct amount of synthetic insulin is given.

Unfortunately our food is often not what it seems — what appears 'healthy' can often not be. And the dangers hide in the smallest things: the hidden sugar and salt and crappy additives.

Make it your business to know what you are eating. Read every packet. You will be surprised by what you will find. I have found milk powder in ham, sugar in pasta sauce and beef fat in lollies. I follow a simple food plan. I don't eat gluten or dairy, and very few grains.

I eat breakfast every day without fail. My whole family eats a cooked breakfast every day. Eggs, spinach and bacon are a much better alternative to all the sugar and junk in some cereals and yoghurts.

Because I travel so much, lunch is always different. Salads are easily accessible, for lunches at home I eat leftovers, and in the winter I always have the crockpot filled with soup!

I have reduced the amount of carbohydrates I eat at dinnertime and have found that I sleep a lot better. Eating large meals and eating late at night will not create the best conditions for a peaceful sleep. It is hard to close the factory down when all the machines are still running!

I often think of my body as a factory. If I want it to function properly, I can't bog it down with a big workload.

Be smart about how you run your body factory! Eat breakfast. Arriving at work without food in your tummy is dumb. It's not helping you to be your best.

We are what we eat. Food is energy. If you put good energy in, you will get good energy out.

DO YOU HAVE A DRINKING PROBLEM?

Being hydrated will change your life. For the sake of your sanity and that of everyone around you, please make sure that you keep hydrated.

My children arrive home at three o'clock and they are grumpy and awful. Two glasses of water seems to change everything.

Drink warm water with lemon upon rising every morning. It restores your alkaline balance, hydrates you and gives you a boost of vitamin C. Water that is at 'blood temperature' is much easier for your body to process than cold or hot water. If you give your body hot water it needs to cool it before it can do anything with it, and if you give it iced water it needs to warm it before processing.

So many women that I meet have wrinkled skin and cracked lips and elbows and are spending hundreds of dollars on cream and lotions to moisturise their skin. Water will plump out your skin and make a huge difference to the texture of your face. Good old water will make your skin plump and bouncy. Stay hydrated — drink water every hour that you are awake, every day.

The only difference between a raisin and a grape is hydration.

GET MOVING

I am not a fan of hard-core exercise. To get me moving, I have to be enjoying an activity a lot. For example, I love to dance. I was even an aerobics instructor once, but this was more about motivating people and looking good in Lycra than fitness, if I am honest!

There are a lot of 'shoulds' and guilt around exercise. I think the simple message is just *move*. Move your bits. Move them doing whatever makes you happy. If walking in the bush floats your boat, then do that. If a loud, pumping Zumba class makes you happy, then do that. If stretching in a chilled-out yoga class makes you feel good, then do that.

It is not important what you do, but more important that you do something. And that you do it often.

Someone once told me that if you spend most of your day alone, then working out in a group or gym environment is a great balance. And the reverse is true: if you work with lots of people all day, then a quiet walk or swim alone may be a better option for you.

Physical exercise has lots of benefits — it relieves stress, can clear your head, strengthens your body and improves your overall health and fitness.

Rather than feeling guilty about what you *should* be doing, go and find something that you *want* to do.

REST IS BEST

Six years ago I booked myself into a weekend retreat as a form of compulsory rest. I find that while weekly and monthly balance is not always easy for me to achieve, if I work in 'quarters' I can create a well-rounded 90 days. I prioritise my work, family, children and health into each 90-day period, making sure that each of my priorities is addressed. A whole weekend of rest once in every cycle works really well for me — allowing myself to completely decompress and regenerate rather than just trying to fit it into each day.

After my weekend retreat in the Coromandel, I arrived at a fashion photo shoot in Auckland bright and early on the Monday morning. I was full of smiles and energy, having just nurtured myself for three days. The photographer, whom I had never worked with before, asked me what my secret was. He was grumbling and groaning about it being a Monday and he wanted to know what I was 'on'!

I told him that several times a year I take myself away to rest. He then said, 'Yeah, it's important to do stuff like that, eh? Or one day you wake up and you are an arsehole!' I nearly fell out of the van laughing. He was right. Without the right rest and self-care, we do become arseholes!

I have always fancied the idea of yoga — the serenity and the flexible people looking all calm and bendy. I spent years attending a weekly yoga group, but because I was pregnant on and off for about four years I always found there was more I couldn't do than could. I even got kicked out of one yoga class for being immature!

It was a class filled with older people and quite a lot of hierarchy. When I arrived I was given the option of three available spaces — all other places were 'taken'. People had their regular spots and god help you if you stood in one of them!

I unrolled my mat. We started with some simple forward stretches. The woman in front of me was like one of those vintage teddies — every time she leaned forward she farted. Brrrrrrp. By the fourth forward bend I could not contain myself any longer. I was crying with laughter. Luckily we were down on all fours. I was trying to gather myself when the man next to me leaned over and told me that I was being very immature. Well, that just made it even funnier! There is nothing funnier than farts — whether you are immature or not. I could not control my laughing and I was beginning to snort. The 'mature' man then suggested that I leave!

Restorative yoga, however, is not a bendy competition where you need to become a human pretzel to get attention, and no one cares if your socks and your yoga mat match. It is the practice of deep relaxation that calms the body, relaxes the mind and puts you at total physical and mental ease. It really is the ultimate in being.

The first time I did this, my head was filled with a large speech along the lines of 'What a waste of time. How self-indulgent! How long will this take? What if I get bored?' My head was like an alligator that I was wrestling with. I had to smother it with a blanket to get it to shut up!

I suggest listening to a guided meditation or soft music at home. I find these techniques help to keep me 'on track' — otherwise my head takes off and I am up and attending to 'stuff' rather than restoring my body with rest.

There are many different positions, using blankets and bolsters and cushions that support the body to the point that it can fully relax. Never have I felt so fully rested than after a restorative session. So deeply calm. It really is the ultimate act of self-care. Folding blankets to support every joint in your body, wrapping your feet and snuggling into metres of polar fleece has to be experienced to be believed.

I have taught myself to surrender to rest — to drop down onto that which supports me and let go. Even after a few minutes I can still find I am holding tension in my neck or ankle. It takes quite a bit of effort to rest! But it is worth it. Since I have made restorative yoga part of my week, I have found I get more done, I feel calmer and am nicer to be around.

It has also taught me the importance of rest. We constantly push our bodies past all our warning signs until they literally stop. Resting our bodies and our minds reduces muscle tension, enhances our immune system and reduces blood pressure.

Our pets can teach us so much about restorative rest. I watch my cats, wandering around and flopping down whenever they want to. Lying in the sun, their round bellies rise and fall with deep, rested breath. We run around huffing and puffing, not lying down until we get 'to the end' (of the day or, ironically, of your life!).

Now, my cats do not have a house to run, a business to manage or a partner or children, so obviously it is a lot easier for them to find the time to rest. But it is not about *finding* time. You have to *make* time.

Time is something we rarely find accidentally. Sure, you might get the odd cancelled appointment or early finish which may give you an extra hour here or there, but you cannot rely on found time for your self-care. If you really are keen on improving your quality of life, then rest. Lie down. If it's for 10 minutes in the back of your car at lunchtime or for 25 minutes with a pile of cushions, just do it. Do it daily.

If you cannot find a restorative yoga teacher near you, then there are plenty of resources online. YouTube also has many postures and prop set-ups that you can follow, as well as meditations you can listen to.

OTHER ENERGIES

Without energy, we are nothing. My energy is my most valued possession. Without it I cannot do anything, help anyone or be anything.

Our physical energy comes from the things that we do to our bodies: sleep, food, drink, exercise and rest will all contribute to your physical energy level.

But aside from physical energy there is also emotional energy, mental energy and spiritual energy.

Emotional energy

Your emotional energy is linked to how you feel about things. If you are deeply sad or incredibly angry, then it is often hard to muster much energy. Your emotional self is so tied up in your emotions that there is no energy left for anything else.

So how do you look after your emotional energy? Being assertive enough to not let people treat you badly, to communicate your needs and to teach people the way you wish to be treated are all great places to start.

MY PERSONAL LAWS

1. I AM RESPECTED. I do not tolerate people speaking badly to me, as a partner, a colleague and especially as a mother. I am not going to let anyone that I gave birth to treat me like crap. It does my head in when women let their own children treat them badly. I will not tolerate anyone I physically created being rude or nasty to me. Parenting is a power game, and too many parents have no power. They have four-year-olds demanding their favourite meals, they have 17-year-olds demanding to be picked up at all hours of the night and day. Set some boundaries.

2. I ONLY DO WHAT I LOVE. This stops me feeling resentful and bored and gives me instant energy. No matter how tired you are, if someone gave you a free trip to Fiji you would find the energy to do it. Constantly doing things we don't want to turns us into martyrs and bores.

3. I AM LOVING AND KIND. I have a belief that there are no bad people in the world, only people who make bad decisions or are in bad circumstances. Being kind is an easy thing to do. Think about where other people are coming from. I will give anyone one chance, maybe two. Never three! The truth is that we never really know what other people are going through. Be kind and give people the benefit of the doubt.

4. I DESERVE THE BEST. I spend a lot of time and money on my energy. I spend a lot of money on good food. I don't eat gluten and dairy. I try to eat as much organic food as possible. I sleep a lot. I listen to my body. I have regular bodywork done: massage, healing and reiki.

5. I SAY WHAT I THINK. I believe that there is a personal power speaking your truth. Try saying what you really think, rather than what you think someone wants to hear. My mother-in-law rang up one day to ask me if we would like to come for dinner. I said no. I didn't want to, it didn't suit me and I would be better off having a night at home. She understood. It was a far better option than going to dinner and feeling resentful all night.

Mental energy

This is about how engaged and stimulated you are. For me, mental energy comes from hanging out with stimulating people who make me think deeply. I love to debate ideas and concepts and explore other people's thinking. Reading books is one of my favourite ways to keep stimulated.

So many people I met are not sure what is 'wrong' with them. They feel flat and have no idea what it is they want or need to improve their lives. I think that they are *bored*. They need to learn something new, meet some new people, study something interesting.

Your mental energy is your thinking energy. What do you think about? What interests you? Exploring topics that make you think is a great way to get mentally stimulated.

Spiritual energy

Spiritual energy is huge for me. My spiritual self helps me to feel supported and safe. Whether you believe in a god or not makes no difference.

I believe that we all have a spiritual self — a piece of god living inside us that we can access. This is a non-judgemental, divine energy that guides us (if we are listening!). It is like a pool of love and support living inside you.

Meditating and being still with my spiritual self has taken me a while to master. But once you know how to access this part of yourself you can become very powerful.

Many people are confused about their spiritual self. They may have been raised on a cocktail of religious beliefs, they may have had religion jammed down their throats or they may have no belief in anything at all. For me it started with a sense of curiosity — I wanted to spend some time working out what I actually did believe, who or what I believed in and what forces I felt in my life.

I do not believe that there are any right or wrong answers here. What you believe is what you believe, end of story. But for people who are looking for more, exploring your spiritual self can be very rewarding.

START WITH QUESTIONS LIKE:

- Do I believe in a god?
- What is my god's name?
- Do I believe in life after death?
- What do I believe happens to me when I die?
- Do I believe that there is more to life than what I can see?

As you answer these questions, think about *why* you believe what you believe. Is it really *your* belief or is it just something that you were told to believe and it has stuck?

I have some very spiritual friends who love to explore their beliefs, and some who think I am a total crackpot when I start talking about past-life experiences and 'working with my guides'. I think that exploring your spiritual beliefs is a really important part of learning to know and like yourself.

PHYSICAL EFFECTS

I am fascinated about the impact that your spiritual and emotional energy can have on your physical body. Years of negative beliefs and locked thinking often leads to physical problems.

Louise Hay is the master of this. *You Can Heal Your Life* is the most incredible book. It includes a list of physical ailments and connects them to the feelings that created them. When I first discovered it 20 years ago, I went around asking people about the areas of their body that had pain or disease and looked up what feeling had created that in their bodies — and it was always so bang on.

Sore throats are almost always about being angry and wanting to yell at someone. Urine infections always show up when you are really 'pissed off', and your knees stop working when we become inflexible in our thinking. My kids are now used to it: when they come home from school and say 'My throat's sore', I always ask them who they are angry at. At first they say no one, they just are getting the flu, but then after a bit of thinking they will realise what it is really about.

Years of negative beliefs and locked thinking often leads to physical problems.

169

ENERGY ROBBERS

I love love *love* people. People are my drug. But some people will hook into your energy field and drain the life-force out of you.

We all have an energy field that is dramatically affected by those around us. There is a sign in our lounge that says 'Please be responsible for the energy you bring into this room'. I often have to say to my children 'Out you go. Go and make yourself nice!'

You know how sometimes a person enters a room and you can feel the state of their energy? They feel angry and heavy and everyone suddenly feels uncomfortable.

People vibrate at different levels. Some operate at a high vibration level and some at a low one.

I have taught myself to be aware of the energies around me. In the same way that you might protect yourself from sickness by not hanging out with someone who is sneezing and coughing, you need to be aware of people with crappy energy. You will feel fine at first, but after 10 minutes of being with them you will feel grumpy and flat.

An important part of your learning to look after your energy is protecting yourself from energy robbers. People can contaminate your energy like bad viruses.

ASK YOURSELF:

- Who lifts my energy?
- Who kills it?

ENERGY CENTRES

We all have an energy field that runs around our bodies. It is called an aura.

We all have seven chakras, or energy centres, in our bodies, going from the top of our head to the base of our spine. I was fortunate to learn about these energy fields and centres at quite a young age and am constantly aware of them.

The word chakra is Sanskrit for wheel. They are wheels of life force or energy. When they are balanced and spinning correctly, life is great. When they are out of alignment — either under-active or over-active — they can cause health issues.

There are a lot of things that you can do to support your chakra energy. There are guided meditations that have special sounds that each chakra responds to, and there are auric healers who can help to clear stagnant energy and open up blocked chakras. Blocked chakras can create physical issues over time.

I met a woman at a conference who said she didn't believe in chakras. I asked her why not and she told me that she couldn't see them, so how could she know that they actually existed? I asked her if she believed in wifi or the wind. Neither can be seen, but we understand the impact both things can have!

Each chakra has a colour, a location and an affirmation associated with it. You can say the affirmations first thing in the morning, throughout your day and last thing at night, or write them down to help your subconscious balance the chakra that the affirmation relates to.

The word chakra is Sanskrit for wheel. They are wheels of life force or energy.

Base chakra — *red*

The base chakra is located at the base of the spine. It is all about your physical safety and security, your physical existence. When it is balanced we feel safe and grounded. When it is out of balance we feel fearful and exhausted. This can show up as adrenal or chronic fatigue.

Feeling unsafe in your home or life is exhausting, as you are constantly using up emotional energy. It makes sense that this chakra being out can make you feel depleted and exhausted.

Affirmation: I am safe.

Sacral chakra — *orange*

The sacral chakra is located in the pelvis. It is all about creative energy, sensuality and flow. It allows us to be sexual and confident and to receive pleasure. When it is balanced we feel sexy, confident and desired.

This chakra being out of balance is often the problem for women who have lost interest in sex, as they have started to believe that they do not deserve pleasure. This can show up as loneliness and addiction. Any addiction will give you the sense of pleasure — shopping, drinking and smoking are all ways we try to give ourselves short-term pleasure.

Affirmation: I flow effortlessly with life.

Solar plexus — *yellow*

The solar plexus chakra is located in the navel. It is all about personal power, self-esteem and ambition. It regulates our fear and control. When it is balanced we feel organised and in control. When it is out of whack we feel powerless and find making decisions difficult. This can lead to weight issues or eating disorders. Low self-esteem and digestive issues are also common problems.

Affirmation: I am powerful. I stand in my power.

Heart chakra — *green*

The heart chakra is located in the heart centre. It is about love, acceptance (of yourself and others) and joy. When it is balanced we feel compassionate, happy and authentic. When it is not we can feel jealous, clingy and disconnected. This can show up physically as poor circulation, asthma and heart issues. Breathe in joy, accept others for who they are and work on forgiveness.

Affirmation: I am loved and loving.

Throat chakra — *blue*

The throat chakra is located in the front of the throat. It is all about communication, self-expression and truth.

Many women struggle with speaking their minds and expressing their ideas, and they literally swallow their words. This can lead to sore throats, swollen glands and thyroid issues.

Affirmation: I express myself freely.

Third eye chakra — *indigo*

The third eye chakra is located between the eyebrows. It represents our intuition and purpose. It is about how we perceive the world.

Vision issues, hormone imbalance, anxiety and trouble sleeping are all signs that this chakra may not be spinning correctly. When it is balanced you will feel clear and have good perspective and direction.

Affirmation: I see and I am seen.

Crown chakra — *violet*

The crown chakra is located just above the top of the head. It is your spiritual chakra that connects you with the divine.

Working on this chakra helps to integrate your physical and spiritual self. It helps to regulate your wisdom and imagination. If it is not spinning you may feel lonely and unfulfilled. Migraines and depression are symptoms that this chakra may need some work.

Affirmation: I am connected to all.

TEN WAYS TO IMPROVE YOUR ENERGY

EAT WELL.

We are what we eat. If you eat crap your body will look, feel and behave like crap. Have enough respect for yourself that you only put good fuel in your tank. Your body will be more like a temple and less like a bouncy castle if you feed it well. Foods like gluten, dairy and heavy grains cause inflammation and weigh our bodies down. Small, high-protein meals are a great way of stabilising your blood sugars, helping your body to maintain consistent energy patterns.

MOVE.

I am not a fan of exercise. Running and jumping hurts, and even as a child I avoided PE class like the plague. But I do like to move. Dancing has always been a passion. Stretching and skipping are things that my body responds well to. Find something your body likes to do and do it. Just move. Every day.

DRINK PLENTY OF WATER.

It will make you look and feel gorgeous.

LEARN NEW THINGS EVERY DAY.

Being a life-long learner is what we should all be striving for. Keeping your brain curious and wanting to learn new things will make you interesting and alive. Embrace technology. Learn how things work. Do not turn into an 'old person'. Life is changing so quickly that we need to be constantly up-skilling ourselves. Do not become extinct in your own lifetime because you can't be bothered learning.

READ.

Theodore Roosevelt said 'I am part of everything I have read.' Reading opens your mind, teaches you stuff, challenges your thinking and makes you clever. Go get a book.

PLAN YOUR DAY/WEEK/MONTH.

Planning your life will make it better. Without a plan, life is just a collection of days. Hope is not a plan. You cannot merely hope that you get to the end of the week, the end of the month or the end of the year with everything done. You will need to plan.

LAUGH.

Hang out with fun people. There is nothing better than a good belly laugh, a good joke, a fun movie. Having laughter in our lives needs to be a priority.

SLEEP.

People tell me that they cannot sleep. They need to make sleep a priority. Magnesium deficiency, eating too late and drinking too much coffee or alcohol will all hinder your sleep patterns. Look into what you can do to improve the quality and quantity of your sleep. Buy a new bed, soak in a bath, take sleep supplements. Sleep is just too precious to ignore.

LISTEN TO MUSIC OR PODCASTS.

Music can calm you down, perk you up, make you think and make you happy. Work out which songs motivate you and which ones calm you down. Driving and singing really badly and really loudly is one of my favourite stress-relieving techniques!

TAKE ACTION.

Do something. Do anything! Action will keep the darkness away. When I am feeling blah, I make myself do something. Get up and move. Pay a bill. Phone a friend. Tidy a drawer. Action will improve your energy.

CHAPTER EIGHT

From limited to unlimited

I have a real problem with limitations. Right from a very young age I seemed to have an allergy to being told that I couldn't do something or that something wasn't possible. I even have a problem with the word limited. If I am in a meeting and someone says 'we are a bit limited with this', I want to get up and throw my phone. It's like a trigger word for me!

I remember when I set up my company and my accountant suggested we could call it Lisa O'Neill Limited. I nearly punched him. Imagine putting that word so close to my actual name! What message would that send the universe? That Lisa O'Neill was limited? No, thank you. I know that limited liability companies need to have 'limited' on the end of them, so I suggested I could be Lisa O'Neill Unlimited Limited. He definitely thought I was mental then.

I am not sure if I was born with my allergy to being limited or whether it was my father's big thinking that rubbed off on me. I think it may be the latter, as my little brother Scott is also of the unlimited variety. He trained as a chartered accountant (very sensible!) but now works with large companies advising them on all things clever and business-like.

We are completely different — but also exactly the same. While we are opposites, we have similar thinking. We are both unlimited. He is, of course, more sensible — always trying to get me to do cash-flows and business plans, as my intuitive business style drives him nuts! But we both believe that we are unlimited.

This belief is the greatest gift that my father gave us as children. He was constantly pushing us, expecting more. He believed we were capable of anything and so did we.

Some people tell me that they don't want to pump their children up so that they become unrealistic about life. I think that being human is enough to keep any of us grounded. Teaching your children to believe that they can do anything is more powerful than any education or experience that you can offer them.

Having a deep belief that I am capable of doing anything that I put my mind to has at times been my biggest asset. I don't have to consider whether I can do something or not, I only have to think about what it is that I want to do.

What would you do if you believed that you could do anything? If you had no limits? We live with limits every day — limited money, limited time, a limited number of people that we know — but this does not mean that we have to limit our thinking.

Allowing ourselves to think 'unlimited' is something I have tried to teach my children. There are so many people in our lives who tell us what we cannot do. They caution us to be careful. To calm down.

All these blankets will eventually dampen the fire. But I like to fan the fire! Here are my favourite questions for people to encourage people to un-limit themselves:

- What would happen if it all went perfectly?
- How would you feel if you achieved that?
- How will you know that you have been successful?
- How bad do you want it?

GOOD INTENTIONS

Too many people are happy to accept mediocrity — they settle. There are two reasons why people have low standards. They either do not believe that they deserve the best or the biggest, or they are too lazy to do the work required to get it.

Setting an intention of what you want and then throwing all your energy at it is the way to get stuff done. Decide. Then Do.

Deciding what you want is critical. Say it out loud. Put a stake in the ground and go for it. But just deciding won't get you the whole way — you will then need to do whatever needs to be done to get you there. The amount of energy you need to give it is determined by how badly you want it.

Imagine that you wanted to compete at the Olympics. The first step would be telling other people. You need to have the balls to say 'I want to be an Olympic athlete'.

You then open yourself up to all the opinions of others and to having to listen to what they think. Surrounding yourself with people who are either crazy-positive or who totally believe in you is key at this point! Hit the positive people first. Telling your big want to someone negative or full of fear won't work.

Once you have made your public declaration of what you are doing, you need to remove any doubt. You will, of course, have doubt but just block it out for a while! The best way I find to do this is to turn the 'I *want* to be an Olympic athlete' statement into an 'I am *going* to be an Olympic athlete' statement. As I mentioned earlier, the power of 'I am' is incredible. When your mind hears 'I am', it believes you. It buys into your story.

Think of something that you want to be or do. Say out loud: 'I *want* to be a _____.'

Now say out loud 'I *am* a _____.' Often this will bring up some emotion. You may get a lump in your throat. You may feel sick. You may want to cry. You may cry! Use that emotion as a sign that you are on the right track.

If your body doesn't react, you may not be on the right track.

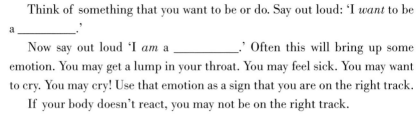

A while ago I was told about a business school in Australia, Thought Leaders Business School, that helped 'clever people be commercially smart'. I wanted to go. I wanted to be a part of a community of people achieving and inspiring others.

My first thought was that it seemed expensive. That was the first block that my head came up with. Having never been scared of spending money to make money, I trampled all over that one.

I started saying to people that I wanted to go to this business school in Australia. The reactions that I got were 'It's a lot of money', 'It will be a lot of work', 'You will be away even more', 'You don't have time to fit in anything else'.

As soon as I turned it into an 'I am' — 'I am going to go to a business school in Australia', people started saying 'Good for you' and 'That sounds amazing'. Because I had decided and put my stick in the sand, they all said supportive things.

When I arrived for my first session at Thought Leaders Business School, the creator of the programme, Matt Church, came to welcome the little group of newbies. He walked in, introduced himself and then said 'Congratulations, you are now on the wrong side of a whole lot of work.' He was not offering us a magical bullet into a successful life — he was offering us the chance to do a lot of work and see a lot of results.

Doing the work is the key. It's the key to everything. If you decide you want to compete at the Olympics, you had better get up early and train. You're not going to get there lying on the couch with a bag of chips. The same applies to anything that you are doing. You need to do the work.

I have always wanted to write a book. I love writing and wanted to be an author. After I wrote my first book, *Look Gorgeous Be Happy*, I received some lovely feedback. One of the comments I heard a lot was from people saying how much they wanted to write a book. They asked me how I found the time. I just did. I decided to write a book and got writing.

If you want to write a book, you need to get up and start writing. You need to do the work. I stopped watching TV. I stopped reading magazines. I wrote and I wrote.

Some days it was really hard. Having committed to my publisher, the pressure to 'perform' was huge. I got tired. I got grumpy. Sometimes I wanted to stop. What got me through all that was focusing on the feeling of completing the book. The feeling of holding my book in my hands. The pride I would feel in my achievement. Focus on the feeling of how you want to feel. Women often comment that I am lucky — lucky to have an amazing job that I love, lucky that I have a successful business doing something that is so much fun.

It is not about luck. I know what I want and I work hard to get it. It is all about want it, don't doubt it, work it. Or decide, believe, do. All three steps are critical.

1. STATE WHAT IT IS YOU WANT.

Deciding is the first bit. What do you really want? And don't panic — you can always change your mind. I have often thought that I wanted something and then halfway in realised that it wasn't really what I wanted. It's OK to change your mind.

2. ALLOW NO DOUBT.

Believe that it is possible. See yourself doing it. Don't listen to doubters. Their opinion doesn't matter.

3. DO THE WORK.

Get busy. Do one thing every day that will bring you closer to your goal. Get rid of excuses. Stop thinking and start doing. One foot in front of the other, every day.

LIVING 'AS IF'

Shifting your thoughts and energy to acting 'as if' is a great way to expand your thinking.

If you want to be something, start living like it is possible. It is the theory of dressing for the job you want. When you start dressing for the job you want, people believe it. You believe it. You get the job. You start to create the energy around what you want when you live as if.

We have all heard of 'fake it until you make it'. And that doesn't mean being fake — what you are doing is faking the energy around you. And then you start to create it. You start to look successful, you start to act successful and then boom! You *are* successful.

If you want to be something, start living like it is possible.

THE REASONABLE STICK

I was telling my brother, an accountant, that I had been asked to speak at a big event. He asked how much I was charging them and I told him that I didn't know. I needed to work out a price and send it to them. He said, 'How much do you want?' I meekly said, 'I don't know' and he said, 'Bullshit! How much do you want?'

He kept asking me this same question while I got all flustered. He asked me if I would like to be paid a million dollars for speaking at this event. I laughed and said, 'Yeah, right!' He said, 'Just say a number — tell me what you think you would like to be paid and then we can beat it with the reasonable stick.'

I had never heard of the 'reasonable stick' before but I really liked it. To be paid one million dollars for a keynote speech. Was that reasonable? Maybe for Sir Richard Branson or Bill Clinton. Not reasonable at this point for Lisa O'Neill!

Good speakers get paid good money. Money that seems huge as an hourly rate. But it is more than that. The speech that you give for one hour is a result of all of that person's years of research, years of experience, years of reading. You are paying for the expertise of that person. Just like when we go to see a medical specialist — we are not just paying him or her for 30 minutes of their time, we are paying for the years of training, experience and expertise that they have brought to that 30 minutes.

In a world where everything seems to have gone a bit mad, I think that everyone needs a reasonable stick. This is not to limit you, but to allow you to think big and then bash a bit of reality into your thinking! Think unlimited but carry your reasonable stick at all times.

What we get paid, what we can do and what we want to do are all things that the reasonable stick can help you sort out.

I love to say yes to opportunities. People are my drug. I find it really hard to say no to exciting opportunities. So I use my reasonable stick to help me with this. I think about all the things that I want to do, then I ask myself if this is reasonable for someone who cares about herself and her family. Is it reasonable to book five conferences in one week and then arrive home so exhausted that I can barely speak to my family? No, it is not.

BEING BIG YOU

So what are your limits? Where are you playing small in your life?

Playing small is of no use to you or anyone around you. I get insanely frustrated by people's limited thinking, with the list of reasons and excuses that they have for why something will not work or why they cannot do something. American author Marianne Williamson wrote:

> Your playing small does not serve the world. There is nothing enlightened about shrinking so that other people will not feel insecure around you. We are all meant to shine, as children do . . . as we let our own light shine, we unconsciously give others permission to do the same.

People playing small is one of my biggest gripes. You have been given a body, a mind and a precious life — what is *big* you going to do? Big you is the shiniest, sparkliest, brightest version of you. It is not the tired, grumpy, limited, small you.

I meet so many women who want more, to do and be more, but they won't get out of their own bloody way. They are full of reasons why thing won't work instead of running off down the road with just one reason why it will.

Big you is limitless. Big you is the answer to the question 'What would you do if you knew you couldn't fail?'

I have to admit, sometimes my limitlessness trips me up. Sometimes you will come across things that you cannot actually do — you can't get other people on board with an idea, or there is something outside of your control that you cannot change.

Whenever I am faced with a situation that I can't do, I ask myself two questions:

- Do I really want this?
- If I could do it, how would I do it? What would I do?

Letting yourself imagine you doing it gives you the power to make it more of a reality. Too many people give up before they even start. They give up in their heads.

ASK YOURSELF:

- What does big me look like?
- Where does big me live?
- What sort of people does big me hang out with?

Imagine the biggest, grandest version of yourself.

Only you can hold yourself back.

CONTAMINATING OR CONTRIBUTING?

In order to be the biggest, grandest version of you, you will need to get some big energy. You will need to get a plan. And you will need to get rid of a few people.

It is important that you work out who is contaminating your life and who is contributing to it. People who are contributing will add value: they will improve your life, lift your energy and make you feel better.

People who are contaminating will drag you down, point out all the things that won't work and generally bring down your buzz.

None of us has time for energy robbers. Avoid them. Do not answer their calls, do not meet them for coffee. Protect your energy from those who might contaminate it.

You will need to get some big energy.

Surround yourself
with people who
see your value and
remind you of it.

— unknown

CHAPTER NINE

Loving YOU

Imagine hanging out with your best friend every day. How much fun would that be — being with someone who had your best interests at heart, who supported you and was nice to you — each and every day?

Now think about how you would feel if you hung out with someone who was constantly telling you off, someone who commented negatively every time you did something and someone who told you you looked fat and ugly at every opportunity . . .

Many of you are living this second scenario. The person that you are hanging out with who is so hard on you is *you*! You expect too much, doubt your own abilities and have little belief in your own self.

Becoming your own best friend is essential to living your life well. If you smoke, binge-drink, overeat, let people treat you badly and always put yourself last, then you may be lacking self-love.

ASK YOURSELF:

- Out of 10, how much do I like myself?

When a woman
becomes her
own best friend,
life is easier.

— Diane Von Furstenberg

SELF-TALK

The way we talk to ourselves is very telling. Stupid bitch. Ugly. Fat cow. We have all left a room and started telling ourselves off. How many times have you heard the words 'You are such an idiot' and realised you are alone? That is *you* talking. *You* being hard on yourself. *You* being a bitch . . . to *you*!

Ultimately we want to get to a place where we are saying to ourselves 'Well done, you did so well', 'You look lovely', 'You're amazing' — just like you would say to a friend who had done something well or looked good. This is a huge step from constantly telling yourself off and the self-bullying that may be going on in your head right now.

The place to start is gentle. Remind yourself that you are going the best that you can. 'You tried', 'Good on you for giving it a crack' and 'Nice job' are all a great start. If you cannot praise yourself, please at least be gentle with yourself.

Louise Hay is the queen of self-love and created the concept of 'mirror work'. This was her method of teaching people to have a deeper relationship with themselves, to like and appreciate themselves.

The first time that you talk to yourself in a mirror you will feel ridiculous. You will be worried someone will catch you and lock you up!

From very early in our lives we receive messages face to face that we absorb. Teaching yourself the messages that you need to hear by speaking directly to yourself in a mirror is a way to reprogram all the negative things that we have absorbed throughout our lives.

This is how I do it. I decided many years ago that I was going to be my own best friend. I decided that I would greet myself in the same way I would greet someone that I liked. I say 'Hi' and I even wave! I waved at myself in a shop mirror one day and a shop assistant saw me — I am sure she thought I had gone completely mad!

Start small. Start with a wave and say hi. Louise Hay suggests looking deeply into your own eyes and saying 'I love you. I truly love you.' This might sound easy but, trust me, it is very confronting when you are looking into a mirror.

Having spent 25 years dressing women and hanging out in changing rooms, I have come across so many women who cannot even make eye contact with themselves. They are not able to look directly in a mirror. Women often cry in changing rooms. They cry because they are disappointed, they are exhausted and they do not like what they see.

Start by looking at something that you do like. Find a physical part of you that you like. Look at it. Stare at it. Love it.

Once you have that sorted, find another bit. Keep looking and finding positive things to say and think about your bits.

ACCEPT YOUR AGE

You have two choices: you can be old or dead. I choose old. Being old is a wonderful thing if you consider the alternative!

I know that dealing with the reality of age can be difficult for so many women. Saggy boobs, lumpy tummies and wrinkled necks are not something that we necessarily enjoy. Body gratitude is the answer — being grateful and constantly reminding ourselves about all the wonderful things our bodies do and are.

Three years ago a good friend of mine had a stroke. He was fit, healthy and didn't drink or smoke, so it was a complete shock to both him and everyone around him.

I sat for weeks in the hospital with him and was amazed by how much of what our bodies do we take for granted. Simple things like picking up a spoon and getting it to his face became a major activity. Walking became something that took huge concentration and effort.

I am in awe of the strength it takes for people to deal with injury, disability and illness. Knowing that my children have to deal with a pancreas that doesn't work properly makes me so grateful every time I open my mouth to eat that I do not have to weigh and measure my food and inject the correct amount of insulin, like they have to. My body naturally works all that out for me.

Eighty per cent of us get the body we deserve. If we have looked after our bodies, then we get better use of them for longer. If you have wrecked your body, then you have to deal with the damage. Be nice to your body. Treat it like a friend.

WHAT ARE YOU GOING TO LOOK LIKE IN 10 YEARS?

This is an interesting question that is worth thinking about. If you are eating a lot of highly processed foods and snacks, then chances are in 10 years you could be carrying a lot of extra weight. If you are running around at a crazy pace, never taking any time to rest, then you might find you end up adrenally exhausted.

Think about where you may be heading and what you would do about that if you truly cared about yourself and your body.

Now, what are you going to do about it?

ACKNOWLEDGE YOUR TENANTS

For those of us who have had the privilege of having babies you will know only too well that it takes its toll on your body. The stretch marks, the flabby skin, the varicose veins . . . all added bonuses for being fertile!

Look at them as badges of honour — you got these things while creating life. You are a bloody miracle producing a miracle. How cool is that? Thank god that there are inventions like body oils (for stretch marks), compression shape-wear (for flabby tummies) and hosiery (for varicose veins) that help us to wear our badges!

GOING UNDER THE KNIFE

People often ask me how I feel about plastic surgery and corrective procedures. My theory is if you want to do it, can afford it and have researched it, then go for it.

I have had friends who have had breast reductions, breast implants, tummy tucks, eye lifts, Botox and laser surgeries. They have all gone in eyes wide open, handed over cash and are delighted with the results.

I believe that it is our right to be in charge of our bodies and that if you don't like something then do something about it. Pick the thing that you don't like — the thing that is stopping you from living your life well — and get it sorted.

But do not do everything. People who look like plastic dolls are not nice to look at and in my experience are never happy. I think that there is a fine line between doing something out of self-love and doing something out of self-hatred.

Having had four babies and now being closer to 50 than 40, the part of my body that I am least keen on is my FUPA. FUPA stands for Fat Upper Pubic Area. It is the pouch that appears under your belly button. (Warning: do not Google this word! You will get some very ugly images!)

I am a fan of shape-wear but packing everything into a compression garment can give you a judder-bar effect once dressed.

The cost of having my FUPA fixed is around $25,000. My stomach muscles, which have been separated by carrying large babies, would be stitched back together and reinforced, creating an internal girdle which would help my posture, back and organs. And while there are risks with a large procedure like this, the benefits are huge: being able to wear garments without tight layers underneath, feeling confident in clothing and not being restricted to wearing things that are flattering to my FUPA!

However, I do not have $25,000 to spend on my body at the moment, nor do I have the time it takes to recover from major surgery. If I was a rugby player who ruined my knee playing rugby, then ACC would pay for me to have it rebuilt. I know that it was my choice, but my body has been ruined by having four children . . . I just need to find a sponsor to have it rebuilt!

My point is that if you want to have something fixed and are prepared to suffer the medical and financial consequences, then away you go. Do not let judgement stand in your way. Likewise, do not judge other people's decisions to have their bits altered. Do what makes you happy. Just do it out of love for yourself.

LOVE HOW YOU DRESS

Once you start to truly like yourself, you will not want to wear clothes that you no longer like. You will want to feel amazing and look amazing. Too many women get stuck waiting to lose weight or to earn more money before they allow themselves the luxury of wearing things that they love. I have worked with many women who already have the gorgeous clothes but don't feel 'worthy of wearing them'.

Buy clothes for now. Not for when you are smaller. Buy what you love. Look for fabrics that feel amazing and colours that make you feel good.

Buy clothes for now. Not for when you are smaller.

LEARNING ABOUT YOURSELF

Part of learning to like yourself is to learn about yourself.

ASK YOURSELF:

- What do I like?
- What are my opinions?
- What are my broken records? What stories am I stuck on?
- What do I no longer care about?

You might find that you need to let shit go. We all have broken records — stories that we tell people over and over again. Stories about our illness, stories about the person who wronged us.

You can't cancel the past. Everything in the past has brought you to where you are today, so be grateful and move on.

Change your mind. Sometimes that is the only power we have. I believe that if you are not changing your mind often, then you are not using it properly.

When you decide to be your own best friend, you decide to be gentle with yourself. To not expect too much, to go easy on you . . .

If you do nothing else other than breathe some days, then that is enough.

If you make a mistake, then laugh and move on.

Life is not that serious! In fact, it is very temporary and terminal.

Being your own best friend is vital. You have no choice other than to spend time with yourself. If you are going to spend time with yourself and enjoy it, then you need to make yourself interesting. Make yourself interesting, make yourself fun, make yourself lovely.

Respect, admire, forgive, accept and nurture yourself!

When you start to call the shots and start to like your body, your home, your family and your self, you can truly say that you love your life.

The bonus is that people who love themselves get what they want. They make themselves a priority in their lives. Their life improves.

Louise Hay says that love is having a deep appreciation for something. Have a deep appreciation for yourself. Love yourself. All of yourself. Appreciate who you really are.

LOVE YOUR DAY

Take yourself on a date.

ON MY PERFECT DAY

I would wear _____

I would visit _____

For breakfast I would eat _____

I would spend time with _____

For lunch I would eat _____

I would go to _____

For dinner I would eat _____

I would buy myself _____

I would listen to _____

CHAPTER TEN

Life hacks

Sometimes it's the little things that can make your life so much easier. If you need a bit of a pick-me-up or a quick fix, try a few of these 'life hacks'.

MAKEUP

- A bold matte lipstick is the quickest way to lift your face and make you look — and feel — brighter and more cheery.
- When choosing a lipstick, hold it up against your face. Choose a colour that 'pops' and stands out against your skin tone.
- A matte lipstick can work well as a blush on the cheeks if used sparingly and blended well.
- Use an old, clean mascara wand and a small amount of hairspray to keep eyebrows in place.
- Mineral powder mixed to a paste with a small amount of water is a great concealer.
- Wash your makeup brushes in shampoo and then rinse them with a little conditioner to keep them soft.
- To stop lipstick getting on your teeth after applying, put your finger into your mouth then pull it out. This removes any lipstick from the inside of your lips.
- Soft coral blush will make you look younger and healthier.

HAIR

- Find a hairdresser that you like. Go often. Do not neglect your hair — bad hair makes you look unkempt and uncared for.
- Cornflour rubbed into your scalp is a brilliant dry shampoo. Place a small amount on your fingertips and rub it in at the roots.
- Sleeping on a firm pillow will stop your hair from getting messed up overnight.

ACCESSORIES AND JEWELLERY

- Decorate yourself. Sparkly earrings will draw attention to your eyes.
- Choose either statement earrings or a necklace — you will look like a Christmas tree if you try to do both at once.
- Always carry a scarf. They can protect your hair from bad weather, cover stains on your top and keep your neck warm.
- Never put accessories on before you use hairspray. The residue will build up on necklaces and earrings.

CLOTHING

- Regularly dye your favourite black clothes to keep them looking new. You can buy easy-to-use fabric dyes from the supermarket.
- Keep a list of items you are shopping for in your wallet — jeans/red high heels, etc. If you find yourself with an hour spare in town you can put it to good use!
- If stuck for what to wear to a special occasion, wear an old dress but buy new shoes and accessories. If you're going to a wedding, wear a plain dress that you already own and buy a hat and matching new shoes.
- Wearing one colour from head to toe will lengthen you, making you look as tall and slim as possible!
- Wearing navy boots with jeans will lengthen your leg.
- V-necks will lengthen your neck.
- Avoid collars if you have a short neck.
- A simple paper clip will change a normal bra into a racer back.
- Sticking a small panty shield in the armpits of silk garments will stop the fabric being damaged by the chemicals in your deodorant. This can also be useful to help with excessive perspiration.
- A safety pin in the seam or hem of a dress will stop static cling by earthing the static energy.

SHOES

- Fix scuff marks on patent black leather shoes using black nail polish.
- Give suede shoes or boots a rub with a natural hairbrush to lift the pile.
- Always spray suede shoes with suede protector before wearing. Respray four times a year.
- At the end of each winter, take your boots and shoes in to be reheeled by a cobbler.
- Hang long boots on clip clothes hangers in your wardrobe.
- If storing long boots standing up, place a rolled up magazine inside each one.

TRAVEL

- To maximise space when packing, tightly roll all clothes rather than folding.
- Use a large pill container to store earrings and small necklaces. It keeps them organised and stops them getting tangled up or damaged.
- Use disposable shower caps to cover shoes in your suitcase.

- Use 'cell bags' or zip-lock plastic bags to keep lingerie/socks/underwear items separate in your suitcase.
- Put scarves, sleepwear and T-shirts into shoes and boots to pack them firmly. This stops them getting creased and damaged.
- Hair straighteners work well to iron collars and lapels when on the road.

EVERYDAY HACKS

- Set an alarm on your phone for 15 minutes before the time on your parking meter runs out. Saves you money on parking tickets!
- Get up early. Half an hour less sleep will be worth it when you are ready and organised for your day. There is nothing worse than being tired, unorganised and late. Just pick tired and sort the rest.
- Each month, spend some time planning for any birthdays or important occasions coming up in the next month. Having gifts and cards sorted ahead of time eliminates so much stress and the guilt of forgetting!
- Carry a list of birthdays by month in your phone or wallet. This acts as a reminder and saves time when shopping for gifts.
- Have a meeting with yourself — at least one each week. Write down everything that you have to do, everything that you want to do and everything that you need to do. Clear your head and get it on paper.
- Start a present cupboard and a card box — it saves so much time when you can buy cards and gifts in advance and just select the right one at the appropriate time.
- Make sure you have at least one really fun and exciting thing to look forward to each month in your calendar.

HEALTH HACKS

- Eat a cooked breakfast. Beginning your day with a sweet bowl of high-sugar cereal or sugar on toast is not a good start. Get some protein on board.
- Rinse your mouth with lukewarm water every morning. It removes the toxins from your tongue and will improve your overall health. Scrubbing your tongue with your toothbrush will also help.
- Visit an osteopath or chiropractor four times a year to stay balanced.
- Set an alarm to remind yourself to go to bed! It's way more proactive than just setting one to wake up.
- Keep a diary of how many hours you sleep each night. Missing one hour each

night from the recommended eight hours' sleep we should all get will give you a sleep debt of a whole night over the period of one week!

- A quick hot bath in Epsom salts will remove toxins and add magnesium to your body. Have the water as hot as possible and stay in for only 10 minutes.

BOOK LIST

I love to read. I love motivational books that open my mind and push my thinking.

Here is a list of the most inspiring books that I have read over the past few years. I read Louise Hay's book *You Can Heal Your Life* when I was 18 years old and I believe that everyone would benefit from reading it. Even if you never look at any of the other books in this list, at least please read *You Can Heal Your Life*.

- *A Pace of Grace: The Virtues of a Sustainable Life*, Linda Kavelin Popov, Penguin, 2004
- *A Return to Love: Reflections on the Principles of "A Course in Miracles"*, Marianne Williamson, HarperCollins, 1992
- *Authentic Success: Essential Lessons and Practices from the World's Leading Coaching Program on Success Intelligence*, Robert Holden, Hay House, 2011
- *Authentic Woman: A Guide to Beauty, Body and Bliss*, Leslie and Susannah Kenton, Vermilion, 2005
- *Be Happy!: Release the Power of Happiness in YOU*, Robert Holden, Hay House, 2009
- *Big Magic: Creative Living Beyond Fear*, Elizabeth Gilbert, Bloomsbury Publishing, 2015
- *Change Your Life Without Getting Out of Bed*, Sark, Simon & Schuster, 1999
- *Conversations with God, Book 1: An Uncommon Dialogue*, Donald Neale Walsch, Penguin, 1996
- *Daring Greatly: How the Courage to Be Vulnerable Transforms the Way We Live, Love, Parent, and Lead*, Brené Brown, Gotham, 2012
- *Dying to Be Me: My Journey from Cancer, to Near Death, to True Healing*, Anita Moorjani, Hay House, 2014
- *Enthusiasm Makes the Difference*, Norman Vincent Peale, Cedar Books, 1973
- *Experience Your Good Now!*, Louise Hay, Hay House, 2010
- *Goddesses Never Age: The Secret Prescription for Radiance, Vitality, and Well-Being*, Christiane Northrup, Hay House, 2015
- *Grow — The Modern Woman's Handbook: How to Connect with Self, Lovers, and Others*, Lynne Franks, Hay House, 2004
- *He'll Be OK: Growing Gorgeous Boys Into Good Men*, Celia Lashlie, HarperCollins, 2005
- *It's Not How Good You Are, It's How Good You Want To Be*, Paul Arden, Phaidon, 2003
- *Life is Short — Wear Your Party Pants*, Loretta La Roche, Hay House, 2013
- *Light is the New Black*, Rebecca Campbell, Hay House, 2015
- *Loveability*, Robert Holden, Hay House, 2013

- *Loving What Is: Four Questions That Can Change Your Life*, Byron Katie, Three Rivers Press, 2003
- *Practising Radical Honesty*, Brad Blanton, Sparrowhawk Publications, 2000
- *Radical Honesty: How To Transform Your Life By Telling The Truth*, Brad Blanton, Sparrowhawk Publications, 1994
- *Rising Strong: The Reckoning. The Rumble. The Revolution*, Brené Brown, Spiegel & Grau, 2015
- *Shift Happens! How to Live an Inspired Life . . . Starting from Now!*, Robert Holden, Hay House, 2000
- *Soul Coaching*, Denise Linn, Hay House, 2003
- *Succulent Wild Woman*, Sark, Simon and Schuster, 1997
- *The 7 Habits of Highly Effective People: Powerful Lessons in Personal Change*, Stephen R Covey, Free Press, 1989
- *The Five Love Languages: How to Express Heartfelt Commitment to Your Mate*, Gary Chapman, Northfield Publishing, 1995
- *The Four Agreements*, Don Miguel Ruiz, Amber-Allen Publishing, 1997
- *The Gifts of Imperfection: Let Go of Who You Think You're Supposed to Be and Embrace Who You Are*, Brené Brown, Hazelden, 2010
- *The Greatest Miracle in the World*, Og Mandino, Bantam Books, 1975
- *The Invitation*, Oriah Mountain Dreamer, HarperOne, 1999
- *The Last Lecture*, Randy Pausch, Hachette, 2008
- *The Life-Changing Magic of Not Giving a F*ck: How to Stop Spending Time You Don't Have with People You Don't Like Doing Things You Don't Want to Do*, Sarah Knight, Little, Brown and Company, 2015
- *The Power of Now: A Guide to Spiritual Enlightenment*, Namaste Publishing, Eckhart Tolle, 2004
- *The Seven Spiritual Laws of Success: A Practical Guide to the Fulfillment of Your Dreams*, Deepak Chopra, New World Library, 1994
- *The Sleep Revolution: Transforming Your Life, One Night at a Time*, Arianna Huffington, Harmony Books, 2016
- *There's a Spiritual Solution to Every Problem*, Wayne W Dyer, HarperCollins, 2001
- *Thrive: The Third Metric to Redefining Success and Creating a Life of Well-Being, Wisdom, and Wonder*, Arianna Huffington, Harmony, 2014
- *Tune In: Let Your Intuition Guide You to Fulfillment and Flow*, Sonia Choquette, Hay House, 2013
- *What Are You Hungry For? The Chopra Solution to Permanent Weight Loss, Well-Being and Lightness of Soul*, Deepak Chopra, Rider, 2013
- *You Can Heal Your Life*, Louise L Hay, Hay House, 1984

ABOUT LISA

Lisa O'Neill is a speaker and stylist, and the author of *Look Gorgeous Be Happy: What a Woman Wants*. She is passionate about helping people to live big, fun lives — people from all walks of life. Lisa works with large companies and self-employed business owners, and she mentors individuals who want more from their lives.

Having married her childhood sweetheart, and now raising four children while building a business, Lisa is the 'queen of the juggle'. A talented multitasker, Lisa has the ability to inspire, and gives practical advice on how to live a life you love.

Lisa has been a television presenter, a fashion editor, a marketing manager and an art director, and spends most of her time these days as a professional speaker. She believes in less housework, more moisturiser and bigger knickers. She loves glitter and big skirts and anything a little bit fancy.

See more at www.lisaoneill.co.nz or follow her at:
www.facebook.com/lisaonNZ

RANDOM HOUSE

UK | USA | Canada | Ireland | Australia
India | New Zealand | South Africa | China

Random House is an imprint of the Penguin Random House group of companies, whose
addresses can be found at global.penguinrandomhouse.com.

Penguin
Random House
New Zealand

First published by Penguin Random House New Zealand, 2017

10 9 8 7 6 5 4 3 2 1

Design by Emma Jakicevich © Penguin Random House New Zealand
Cover photograph by Mark Barber

Text on page 45 from *He'll Be OK: Growing Gorgeous Boys Into Good Men* © 2005.
Published by HarperCollins, Auckland.
All rights reserved. Reproduced with permission of the author's daughter.

Text on page 113 from 'The Invitation' © 1999. Published by HarperOne, San Francisco.
All rights reserved. Reproduced with permission of the author. www.oriah.org

Text on page 184 from *A Return to Love: Reflections on the Principles of "A Course in
Miracles"* © 1996. Published by HarperOne, San Francisco.
All rights reserved. Reproduced with permission of the author.

Flower imagery © Le Do and BoxerX/Shutterstock.com

Prepress by Image Centre Group
Printed and bound in China by RR Donnelley Asia Printing Solutions Ltd

A catalogue record for this book is available from the National Library of New Zealand.

ISBN 978-0-14377-044-2

penguin.co.nz